Image at the Top

Crisis and Renaissance in
Corporate Leadership

Image at the Top

Crisis and Renaissance in Corporate Leadership

Richard S. Ruch
and
Ronald Goodman

This is a special edition prepared for The Presidents Association

THE FREE PRESS
A Division of Macmillan, Inc.
NEW YORK

Collier Macmillan Publishers
LONDON

The Free Press
A Division of Macmillan, Inc.
866 Third Avenue, New York, N.Y. 10022

Collier Macmillan Canada, Inc.

Printed in the United States of America

printing number

1 2 3 4 5 6 7 8 9 10

Library of Congress Cataloging in Publication Data

Ruch, Richard S.
    Image at the top.

    Includes index.
    1. Communication in management—United States.
2. Executives—United States.   I. Goodman, Ronald.
II. Title.
HD30.3.R8   1983   658.4'095'0973   83–48146
ISBN 0–02–927420–6

CONTENTS

FOREWORD

Productivity. The word itself sounds impersonal. No wonder, then, that so many schemes to achieve it have been mechanistic, focusing more on the system than on its human components.

Today, there is a reawakening to the importance of those human components—in all their complexity. Our utilization of technology has outstripped our ability to mine the human potential in the workplace, and management today is rushing to right the balance.

In a recent study of management training programs in major corporations, Robert Hahn, director of the Institute for the Management of Lifelong Education at Harvard, found "a clear emphasis on process, rather than on content." Among the top 10 training goals for managers, Hahn found, are development of:

- the ability to interact easily and productively with others

- the ability to listen effectively

- the ability to communicate ideas orally

- tolerance and trust in relations with others

Whether these goals are being realized, however—whether managers are developing and exploiting these abilities—is less a function of what they can do than of what the business climate in which they operate allows and demands.

The climate of an organization, the authors of this book have found distinctly in both their research and their consulting work, is set at the top. People in an organization are most influenced by how they perceive the top management of the firm. And people outside the organization, too, see it largely as its top management presents it.

Productivity gains today result when the hearts and imaginations of every individual human being on whom an organization depends are sparked. It is only the man or woman at the top who can, consistently, send out these sparks. This book can help you, in that top position, create for your own organization the competitive advantage: the full utilization of the human resources which are there for the inspiration.

Jane G. Bensahel, Senior Editor
The Research Institute of America

PERSONAL NOTE FROM THE AUTHORS

CORPORATE AMERICA is in serious trouble. No need to dwell on the recession, high unemployment, or the toll of human suffering fueled by economic dislocation. Our national and industrial ills strike to the core of the human spirit. Our most precious national resources—the creative ideas and ingenuity that built our industrial might, the grass-roots use of the ol' bean to figure out the better way, to plow a straighter furrow—are being dulled and thwarted. The enemy, as we have long been warned, is us.

The good ideas of the people at the bottom of the totem pole of working America are no longer moving up the channels of communication to the people at the top, and messages sent downward are not received. Our factories and offices are filled to the brim with alienated men and women who, in fact, hold many of the right answers. But we are not listening. Amidst the massive outpouring of data, computer printouts, and television's tasteless wasteland, people are starving for authentic, caring human communication for the workforce. Babel's towering flow of noncommunication has all but drowned us in a sea of information. Having arrived at the Information Age, we find ourselves adrift.

Four years ago, a story in the *Kansas City Star* brought us together. This one piece of news changed our lives, and it is our hope that this book may lead to a change in yours. The story dealt with Richard's analysis of research among General Motors assembly line employees, showing that workers' perceptions of the top managers at the helm of GM—the "image at the top"—had a more profound impact on job attitudes than any other single factor in the work setting. When Ron, a long-time corporate communications counselor, saw that story, he felt that a whole new way to communicate could be developed using the "image at the top" as the medium through which caring and truthful interaction could be created.

Richard urges putting love back into the workplace. Ron speaks of the urgency of truth telling and has made a career of it. As with most powerfully fundamental ideas, our thesis is not so much a new invention as a return to basic wisdom as old as the Bible and as new as the latest theory of managerial leadership. This is the basis of the Goodman–Ruch partnership.

It is the same partnership that we write of in this book. Educators must join with business executives in a new Renaissance of leadership to apply open and honest communication as the means to achieve the moral and material prosperity we all yearn for.

To commit to that business philosophy ourselves, Ron took a leave from the corporate suite as a visiting university professor. Richard was drawn into Ron's practice to apply the new research findings to the thorny problems of real companies with snarled lines of noncommunication.

The story of what we learned and seek to pass on is told on the following pages.

Richard S. Ruch, Ph.D.
Dean, School of Business
  Administration
Rider College
Lawrenceville, NJ

Ronald Goodman, APR
R. M. Seaton Distinguished
  Visiting Professional
Kansas State University
Manhattan, KS

THOUGHTS ON TEAMWORK

WE GRATEFULLY ACKNOWLEDGE the caring help and thoughtful insights of many persons who stopped what they were doing in the pursuit of their lives to lend us assistance. Hundreds of individuals in factories and offices across America opened their minds and hearts to our questions and helped us listen to their answers.

Two consulting colleagues have served as navigators as we charted our course, and each has generously contributed valued expertise. Their faith was comforting as we looked into the distant unknown. G. Frances Stone, Vice President—Corporate Services at Merrill Lynch Pierce Fenner & Smith, chartered financial analyst, and consulting economist, reviewed all of our statistics and is responsible for the soundness of the economic trend lines we use. Glenn Leggett, retired Vice President for Corporate Communication at Deere & Company and President Emeritus of Grinnell College, told us how it was, selected poetry for us, and wielded his English professor's pen on our manuscript.

Robert A. Lynn, Dean of the College of Business Administration at Kansas State University, and Harry D. Marsh, Head of the Department of Journalism and Mass Communications, encouraged us and willingly provided the use of staff resources to support this project.

A number of American corporations opened their doors to our ideas and methods, enabling us to make personal contact with several hundred American workers at every organizational level. General Motors Corporation provided some of the research data upon which the book is founded. National Tea Company, through Sheldon V. Durtsche, Senior Vice President for Finance, had the vision to see the wisdom of listening to what employees were saying, thinking, and feeling. At Whitaker Cable Corporation, John H. Whitaker, President and Chief Operating Officer, had the courage and conviction about the Doctrine of Open Communication to sponsor our Communication Audit. At American Telephone and Telegraph Corporation, Tapas K. Sen, Division Manager for Work Relationships Research, was an early and strong supporter of our ideas. D. Larry Lemasters, President of American Transtech, Inc., and Robert

F. Santos, Vice President of AT&T's Information Systems Division, embraced and supported our ideas both personally and in their own organizations.

Ronald Goodman expresses to Dorothy Anne Anderson, art therapist, his appreciation for her wisdom and illuminating insight into the human spirit. Richard Ruch acknowledges to Christy Stephenson Ruch his appreciation for her many sensible and logical suggestions.

Lee Ross at Kansas State repeatedly gave assistance beyond the call of duty to get our ideas on paper and, with Candace Hayden, put our thinking through the reality therapy process by giving us their workers' viewpoints. At Rider College, Mildred F. Dill was administrative coordinator of the project. Jane Mayrhofer and Mary Raymond provided the word processing teamwork that kept us on schedule.

PART ONE

Overview

CHAPTER 1

The Present Crisis in American Corporate Leadership

*Let me exhort everyone to do their utmost to think outside
and beyond our present circle of ideas. For every idea gained
is a hundred years of slavery remitted.*

Richard Jeffries

AMERICA'S CORPORATE LEADERSHIP is facing the test of its life.
In the face of a tremendous storehouse of rich natural resources,
brainpower, and human talent that has been the envy of the world
since the production miracles of World War II, our industrial leaders
now stand bewildered. They watch real GNP declining, productivity
dropping, unemployment running to over 10 million, and visions
of a 1929 depression rumbling into the national conscience—while
compensation has risen 53 percent since 1977.

Lagging growth in labor productivity is a relatively easy symptom to measure. The U.S. Bureau of Labor Statistics records productivity increases in manufacturing, which show the United States
slumping badly behind Italy, Germany, France, the Netherlands,
and, of course, Japan, for the last two decades. Putting aside the
technical problems of defining and measuring the concept of productivity, the overwhelming evidence shows that our productivity
growth has not just slowed—productivity has been falling steadily
in the United States since 1950. And as productivity has been headed
toward Death Valley, especially in the last half-dozen years, per
capita GNP has also dropped, while employee compensation has

doubled. Unemployment and the consumer price index have increased dangerously during the same period. These fathomings of our economic ill health are sure warning signals for business, industry, and the nation.[1]

How did we get into such a state? Who and what are to blame?

Underlying causes of our sagging productivity defy easy explanation. Some analysts point to obsolete facilities and an aging capital base, others to the relatively small percentage of national output invested in expanding and upgrading the stock of our productive capital. Edwards M. Deming, who brought western management techniques to war-ravaged Japan, makes this sweeping indictment: "Management has failed in this country."[2]

In human terms, the crisis in American corporate leadership is characterized by large numbers of angry and alienated employees. The human suffering is growing extreme. Job-related suicides are increasing, and recession-based mental health problems are spiraling. Polls conducted by Opinion Research Corporation and by the University of Michigan's Survey Research Center, studies conducted by the Work in America Institute, and uncounted numbers of employee attitude surveys conducted by major U.S. corporations collectively reveal that more American workers are dissatisfied with their jobs now than at any other time in the past 30 years.[3] Curiously, many of the obvious conditions of the workplace have actually improved during that period—shorter hours, better pay, better benefits—yet the enjoyment and fulfillment gained from a positive work experience have all but disappeared from the attitude scales.

The zest is out of work; the much-vaunted American work ethic is not alive and well from sea to shining sea. It exists regionally in happy pockets and small enclaves, but the great heartbeat of a mighty industrial power is running down and the corporate body of America grows pale and wan. Annually and quarterly the trend line of profits is down. Many blue-chip companies are in the red, and more companies have gone bankrupt than at any time since the Great Depression.

Businesses are filing for bankruptcy at the rate of 36 for every hour of the working day, and the tempo is accelerating to the point where it shortly may match the 1933 rate of 100 per 100,000 companies. Four-fifths of all bankruptcies are straight liquidations. Corporate assets are auctioned off and scattered, and thousands of jobs are permanently lost. Deregulation of the trucking industry has pushed 144 trucking firms under since mid-1980, and 28,600 persons lost jobs in that one segment of the economy alone.[4] Such a large number of closings cannot be attributed merely to competition in the trucking industry.

Many famous names are on the list of once proud companies now down the tubes—Braniff International, Wickes, AM International, Saxon Industries, Lionel—and International Harvester is teetering at the brink. Edward I. Altman, a finance professor and chairman of the MBA program at New York University, estimates that 200 of the 2,000 largest industrial companies are potential bankruptcy candidates as evidenced by the weakness of their balance sheets.

Heavy is the burden of the Pension Benefit Guaranty Corporation, a government agency that shores up insolvent retirement plans. Pension experts fear that a few major new bankruptcies could wreck the PBGC.

In diverse ways, business is making decisions today that are cutting into the long-term vitality of the U.S. industrial base and eroding the foundations of our future. In research and development expenditures, the annual increase in spending was sliced from 7.2 percent in 1980 to 3.8 percent in 1982. A McGraw-Hill survey showed that business in 1982 spent only 3.9 percent more on fixed plant and equipment projects than in 1981. Allowing for inflation, that reveals a 4.5 percent decline. Albert T. Sommers, chief executive of the Conference Board, warns, "By cutting into capital investment now, we are bending our country's long-term growth trend down. A very prolonged deferral of investment will cost the country billions of dollars in lost output. It will take a long time to make this up."[5]

Unionization has produced automatic increases in labor costs for many industries. The cost of simply maintaining medical and pension benefits has risen at a double-digit rate each year since the mid-1970s, and surging inflation has prompted many unions to lock on to cost-of-living adjustment clauses with a death grip, resulting in rigid and inflexible adversarial relationships between management and workers. Unionization itself is probably not the culprit. In fact, a 1980 study of the U.S. cement industry showed that unionization had actually led to productivity gains.[6]

The real culprit is a knee-jerk antiunion (and antimanagement, on the part of labor unions) sentiment that has soured the whole industrial relations system in the United States. Instead of working together through these tough times, management and labor in the

United States seem to be moving farther apart. The tension and politicking are getting worse.

Male/female roles in the workplace are also undergoing a revolution, and this too has contributed to the present crisis. Rather than share the best features of their traditional sex roles, men and women executives have too often been unwilling to accept their natural gender traits and work together as coequals. Male managers see their female counterparts as being obsessed with form and the subtleties of expression and appearances. They see women managers as using sexism as a crutch and often misconstruing genuinely innocent behavior and even common courtesies as a form of sexual harassment. Many men say they are afraid to criticize women managers because they tend to overreact and get too emotional. Women managers say of their male counterparts that they treat women differently but they don't *think* they do. They say that men don't provide bona fide help to women who want to grow into the managerial role. Many women say they feel men lack basic confidence in a woman's natural abilities as a manager.[7]

The result is that men and women managers often do not relate to each other supportively in a mutually satisfying work environment. Sexual overtones and sex-bound role ambiguities have weakened the fabric of American corporate leadership at the very time when the nation needs strong and vigorous leaders to cope with a national economic emergency.

This corporate leadership crisis runs deeply into the educational support system provided by collegiate business schools. The gap between what business schools teach and what managers actually need to know is widening. If Edwards Deming is right that management has failed in this country, then a share of the blame must go to the nation's business schools, which for the most part have been unresponsive to the present crisis.

Most business schools spend more time and money on documenting the current economic crisis than on using their brainpower in innovative ways to fix business education where it appears to be inadequate. Such areas as interpersonal communication, leadership development, and business ethics are serious weak spots.

Too many of the brightest and best business educators are leaving the hallowed halls of academe (or don't opt for it in the first place), not just for a more adequate salary, but because teaching and research in an often changeless, dull, and stifling environment does not provide sufficient opportunity for intellectual stimulation.

Sadly, our formal educational system does not encourage risk taking. American business schools, although they do some things very well, now threaten to become impersonal credentialing assembly lines. They are turning out graduates who do not know how to communicate and have not been taught the importance of good communication as the essential basis for effective leadership. Too many business school graduates have become so imbued with the desire to quantify all decision making that they have not learned the value of basing judgments on experience in the marketplace— experience gained by talking to live customers or listening to what the people who make channels of distribution work have to say.

And we should not be harsh exclusively with the business schools. Schools of journalism, which purport to teach in the various media known collectively and vaguely as mass communications, are releasing graduates who are presumably trained in the art of communication. But harried communication directors in companies across the land know from first-hand experience that such J-school graduates equate writing with News Reporting 1. Ask them to create some fresh ideas in the form of a persuasive essay and they are numb with incomprehension.

Just as bad, the gap between management research and management practice has also continued to grow. Corporate foundation members are timid about exercising their own good independent judgment. Too much money is thrown after esoteric and ill-defined research projects. The management literature reflects a stagnant loss of new ideas, new concepts, and the development of better ways of managing resources. Very few corporate executives know anything about good research beyond the simple-minded treatment (borrowed as it is from the "hard" sciences) that they may have absorbed from a typically inadequate course called Marketing Research. Similarly, management researchers who have the proper training to conduct scientific research hold an uninformed or jaded view of corporation management. The result is that most of the academic journal articles reporting research studies in management have little to do with the real world of management, though many managers are too easily duped by pedantic scientific rhetoric and scholastic verbal runaround.

But the crisis in American corporate leadership goes much deeper than management research, education, changing male/female roles, the rise in unionization, the loss of work satisfaction, and the lowering of labor productivity. American corporate executives facing the middle years in this decade of the 1980s are wrestling with leadership problems few have ever seen before.

A whole generation of business leaders are in CEO positions with no experience whatsoever in managing in a downside economy. They have been nurtured in an economic environment where anyone could make money and the *in*efficiencies of scale were glossed over by burgeoning earnings that seemed to roll in like the tide. Seeing the tide of economic adversity turn against them, they have precious few role models to study. Not enough of the case study problems in business schools deal with bankruptcy-threatening conditions. Operating managers often are unable to handle well such facts of life as closing down plants and consolidating assets to achieve substantially lower break-even points.

"Small is beautiful" is just a catchy slogan to this generation of managers, so accustomed to legions of corporate staff performing work for them that they have forgotten the essential lessons of managing lean and hungry. While such managers sway off balance and scramble to form strategies to operate their companies in the face of the grimmest recessional economy in memory, other managers, who follow a different set of leadership principles and who never forgot how to use good human communication as the core of their managerial style, are surviving and some are even thriving.

Take Carlisle Corporation in Cincinnati. In a recent year this diversified industrial company had sales of $406.3 million, a 7 percent sales increase, and a 37 percent increase in earnings, with profit margins upped to 8.7 percent from the prior year's 6.8 percent. Return on average stockholder's equity was 29.8 percent, up 2.2 percent. Carlisle's construction material sales rose 42 percent in a weak market for roofing systems. These sales were based on innovative products that are produced by low-cost manufacturing and technological developments achieved according to a management plan clearly communicated in the corporate annual report for Wall Street and all shareowners to see.

Carlisle management operates with a lean headquarters group of only 13 people. Corporate staff functions are reduced to absolute essentials, and power is given to the profit center managers who make decisions based on short-line communication input and close understanding of what the marketplace is saying.

Talking with Malcolm C. Myers, Carlisle's president and CEO, one gets clear insight into how communication is forged into the company's overall business plan as an essential management tool.

We communicate with our people through the planning process. There is a healthy interaction between our corporate group and our divisional presidents. The corporate plan is based on input from each division, and there naturally is a lot of give and take in that dialogue as our annual operating plan and our long-range plans are formulated.

After we have agreed on the plans, we urge each division executive to communicate the plan to every employee. We believe strongly in decentralization and give wide latitude to our managers on how they are going to execute the program we have agreed upon. Some division presidents will hold dinner meetings with their people and discuss our plan in detail. We reveal confidential information to our employees in these meetings, and to protect that type of information, we ask that they make no notes—just listen closely. In some cases our managers will use video tapes if that is more comfortable for them; in others they like to use a series of small-group meetings to emphasize the personal approach. But we insist that every division head meet with *all* of his employees so everyone has equal access to the same information.

Beyond this annual communication process emphasizing the year's operating plan as well as the longer-range program, we encourage all division heads to meet with all their people personally in small groups two and three times during the year. We stress the personal approach, and we want to have an honest and open dialogue with our employees.

We try hard to find out what's on employees' minds. Periodically, we will have consultants come in to do attitude studies in our plants. I have found that the findings generally break down into equal thirds: one-third of what's on workers' minds can be corrected or changed almost immediately, and we do take action. The second third of their concerns usually takes longer to implement, but we do follow through and make those changes. But the final third sometimes covers areas where it is impossible for anything to be done, and we tell them why.

An example of how we work to let people know we care about them is in making an acquisition. When our board and the board of the company to be acquired agree in principle to the acquisition, I will personally visit the prospect company and will talk with the employees to tell them about Carlisle. I know they are concerned about their future, and I try and tell them first-hand what we are all trying to accomplish and the role they can play. I have found this openness is exceedingly well received.[8]

Or take the General Motors dealership, Holm Motor, Inc., in little Ellsworth, Kansas, population 2,840, which just had its best new-car sales year in the 13-year history of ownership by its present management. George Holm, the owner-manager, and his two sons Jeff and Tim work as part of a 12-person team operation.

This is how George Holm decided he wasn't going to join the recession:

> In 1979 when I heard the talk of doom and gloom, interest rates were rising, and I felt we were entering a recession, I called our people together and we had a meeting.
>
> I talked to them about Chrysler's problems and we discussed Braniff Airlines' difficulties, and I told them that we could control our own future. It didn't have to happen to us. If we all decided we were going to work harder and each would carry our own load and we agreed to cooperate and work as a team, we were going to weather the storm.
>
> That's just what happened. We've made money in '79, '80, '81, and in '82 we've had our best year ever. I try and set an example for my people. I am concerned about my people. I care about them, and I try and treat them all as part of a family.[9]

As 1982 drew to a close, George Holm was making plans to buy another GM dealership in Abilene, Kansas, to expand his marketing base. Sharp contrast to the wailing and moaning of most U.S. auto dealers.

Just look at some of the facts and figures facing the auto industry's top executives in Detroit. Imported cars have seized their highest-ever share of the U.S. auto market just by holding their own and watching Detroit itself lose more share of the market. General Motors' August 1982 sales plunged 34 percent from a year earlier. Ford sales were down 24 percent, Chrysler sales fell 33 percent, Volkswagen of America, Inc., sales of U.S.-built cars were down 44 percent, and American Motors sales were off 45 percent. As of fall 1982, the U.S. auto industry had over 250,000 employees laid off or on extended furlough. In fiscal 1980, GM, once considered solid as the rock of Gibraltar and the cornerstone of sound, durable management, had a loss of $762.5 million. This was the largest loss in 60 years of General Motors' history.

Meantime, U.S. auto makers have been forced to watch the skilled managers of foreign auto companies sweep into the U.S. market with well-designed, fuel-efficient, soundly engineered cars until they had chiseled off over half of the U.S. action for under-30 buyers and over a third of the market overall.

The Japanese alone have made off with over 25 percent of the U.S. market. So skilled have been Japanese managers that they not only have taken the lion's share of the Detroit market but have literally captured the imagination of the U.S. consumer. They have outdesigned, outperformed, and outmaneuvered the U.S. auto industry. All this from a tiny country of 118 million people that was rubbled in 1945, its industries reduced to smoking ruins by the devastating air raids dealt by our B-29s operating from Saipan and Okinawa.

James E. Harbour, a Michigan-based management consultant who spent 23 years as a Chrysler manufacturing engineer, calculates that Detroit needs 120 hours of labor to assemble a subcompact car. Workers in Japanese factories need only 60 hours to do the same work functions. Why the difference?

At Toyota, management/worker cooperation, based on management listening to what the workers are saying, is one major answer. While U.S. auto makers are just now waking up to the pure gold in the ideas and suggestions of their workers, Toyota's managers for years have been mining that gold by paying sensitive and respectful attention to the potential inherent in its workforce. This human resource at Toyota produces over a million suggestions annually, or an average of 31 per worker. In a recent year, management accepted 92 percent of the ideas and the company saved $131 million, while achieving an annual productivity increase of 11 percent.

Now, U.S. executives have also seen a little book on the code of the Samurai warrior swordsman become a bestseller in Wall Street, presumably making available to aspiring junior executives, the secrets of the Japanese managerial style. *A Book of Five Rings* by Miyamoto Musashi, originally written in 1600 as a philosophy of warfare, has been resurrected by a smart marketer at the Overlook Press.[10] It has now sold over 120,000 copies in the hardcover edition alone with the seductive suggestion that a reading of the book will somehow transfuse a mystical ancient managerial cult of leadership into American executive suites.

While that book became a bestseller, executives at General Motors entered a state of shock at the revelation of an opinion survey by Yankelovich, Skelly & White that 60 percent of GM salaried employees believed the company turned a profit in fiscal 1980, despite GM's widely reported loss of $762.5 million.[11] GM's mammoth public relations staff had produced a film, "The Battle for Survival" especially designed by senior corporate management to alert GM employees to the ravaging impact of foreign-car imports on the financial position of the corporation and the inherent threat to employee jobs. The film was considered so important to the financial health and future of the company that F. James McDonald, GM's president, personally narrated it. Roger B. Smith, GM's chairman and CEO, was surprised that GM's workers apparently were not believing or paying serious attention to what management at the top was reporting about the company's financial ill health. Alfred S. Warren, Jr., vice president in charge of industrial relations staff at General Motors, then admitted publicly to a *Wall Street Journal* reporter that GM had "a serious problem."

Douglas A. Fraser, the first American union leader to serve on a corporate board (Chrysler), finally acceded to the pressure of other major American corporations clamoring for reconsideration of the oppressive labor rates locked into the then current labor contract with Detroit auto and farm equipment industries. The UAW's Council, meeting in Detroit in November 1981, finally agreed to a new policy of rank-and-file approval to reopen individual contracts and renegotiate local labor rates. It may have been a case of too little and too late.

The dilemma facing thousands of other corporate leaders today is the very same one being examined squarely by the U.S. auto industry CEOs: "How do I communicate my company's real needs and problems to my workforce, my stockholders, consumers, and government when they don't believe what I am saying or won't listen?"

That's both cause and symptom of our leadership crisis.

CHAPTER 2

Image at the Top—
Critical Role of the CEO

*No sadder proof can be given by a man of his own littleness
than disbelief in great men.*

Thomas Carlyle

WHAT EMPLOYEES THINK of top management in their organizations has a powerful influence on employee behavior, quality of work, and, we believe, productivity and profit. This truism, long recognized by seasoned consultants and enlightened managers in American industry, holds a powerful key to the solution of the present crisis in American corporate leadership.

If American corporate managers are to lead the nation's industrial economy to a new high ground of fiscal stability, regain lost markets, and reestablish the competitive edge that once made the U.S. industrial machine esteemed worldwide, they are going to have to pass a hard-nosed, obstacle-laden crash course in effective communication.

Research among blue-collar workers in 10 U.S. General Motors plants, later reconfirmed in a study of Big Eight public accounting firms and buttressed by data from our consulting engagements, has shown that the image at the top affects employees' work attitudes more directly than any other single factor in the work environment. This ongoing research is the backbone of this book.

The GM Employee Survey

A big share of the credit for this research goes to General Motors Corporation, which initiated the original study a decade ago, in November 1972, under the auspices of its Organizational Research and Development Department (ORD) in Detroit and later provided financial support for the continuance of the research. GM has long been noted for conducting and supporting good research in the behavioral areas of management. One of the largest industrial surveys of employee attitudes ever conducted, this one was called, simply, the "GM Employee Survey."

The original survey questionnaire, developed at GM with counsel from the University of Michigan's Survey Research Center at the Institute for Social Research, contained a crushing 128 items and was 13 pages long. The initial sample included nearly 3,500 nonskilled, hourly-rated employees randomly drawn from 14 GM plants around the country. The data were collected between November 1972 and January 1973.

GM's motivation for this huge study sprang from strongly negative public opinion about assembly line work in America, fueled by newspaper and magazine articles that criticized GM for not doing much about it. The popular view that assembly line work was inherently psychologically devastating was gaining widespread visibility and popularity in the late 1960s and early 1970s. The GM Employee Survey was seen by GM executives as a possible means to head off the growing public ill will. One of the project reports stated:

> Due to increasing criticism of car assembly technology in general and GM in particular, members of the GM Public Relations Staff, the Industrial Relations Staff, and the Personnel Administration and Development Staff met in the fall of 1972 to discuss ways of countering these critics-at-large. They agreed that an objective assessment of assembly employee opinions about their work was essential. To this purpose a large-scale survey was conducted over a three month period beginning in November, 1972.[1]

Did it work? Yes and no. Yes, GM did discover something important and essential about worker attitudes, opening the door for some major follow-up research. But no, public opinion about GM and assembly line work was not turned around.

In the familiar fashion of corporate research reporting, GM generalized and simplified the findings. The final report noted that a certain percentage of the employees surveyed were "satisfied," a certain percentage "neutral," and a certain percentage "dissatisfied." While GM researchers did perform some additional statistical analyses of the data, the overall data analysis seemed a bit sketchy, even to some of the GM research staffers. But there was one finding of paramount importance tucked away in the conclusion section of the final survey report:

> Specifically, a people-oriented management system is the one best contributor to high job satisfaction. . . . Management needs to focus its attention on generating a satisfying work environment if they want to bring about constructive changes in the job-related attitudes of hourly employees.[2]

Out of dozens of factors—biographic and demographic characteristics, pay and benefits, work technology, environmental factors—the one thing that more than anything else led to high worker job satisfaction was a *people-oriented management system*. This was a significant and far-reaching finding. GM staff researchers in ORD knew their initial analysis called for further study. They decided to give the data to an outside researcher for further analyses. That's when Richard Ruch got it.

That decision marked the beginning of this book, although we did not know it at the time.

Top Management Was the Key

In both the original GM data analysis and Ruch's primary follow-up analysis, no distinction was made by the researchers between supervisory management and upper management. They were simply looking at the impact of workers' overall view of management on job attitudes. When the data were analyzed more closely, however, it became evident that the employees themselves had answered the management questions differently—so much so that their overall perception of management could no longer be considered a single factor.[3]

Two distinct factors emerged, depending upon whether the word "supervisor" or "foreman" appeared or did not appear in the questionnaire item. A computer program designed to recheck all responses to the management questions confirmed that employees did not consider management to be a single entity at all—their view of supervisory management affected their job attitudes differently than their view of top management.

The employees' view of top management, from the plant manager right up through GM Central Office executives and the chairman himself, had the greatest single impact on worker job attitudes of all the factors studied. In many cases, the workers did not even know the names and faces of these top executives, yet their view of them was the major ingredient in having a positive work attitude.

Managers and management consultants had long thought that top management played a critical role in determining employee attitudes. Now, we finally had the scientific data that clearly confirmed those intuitive judgments.

In fact, the same finding on the critical role of top management has now been reconfirmed with data from two very different industrial settings. Dr. Tapas K. Sen, manager of work relationships research at giant AT&T, has provided survey data collected at AT&T which support the findings of the GM Employee Survey. Dr. Robert Holtfreter at Kansas State University has worked with one of us on another study of job attitudes among professional auditors at the Kansas City offices of the Big Eight public accounting firms. Again in this study, how the auditors viewed top management, in this case the partners in the individual CPA firms, had the single greatest impact on a positive work attitude over all other factors in that work environment.

A special report from Opinion Research Corporation (ORC), released in December 1982, adds still further evidence to the compelling importance of how employees view the top of their organizations. Based on the latest findings of their ongoing survey of the climate of the American workplace, ORC researchers held an all-day strategy briefing for senior managers in New York. Here was their key message:

> Progress in productivity is threatened by top management's retreat from the more open styles achieved in the late 1970's and growing discontent of employees—including middle management. *Employees' dissatisfaction focuses on the company as a whole and on the quality of top management, rather than on the specific job itself.* . . .
>
> In recent years employees have become increasingly negative about various management practices, ORC reports. All employee groups felt that fairness in applying policies and rules had deteriorated. The same was true in rating the companies' responsiveness to employee problems.

In a related trend, *more employees felt that their companies were losing touch with individuals.*[4] (Emphasis added.)

Focusing specifically on top management, the ORC researchers found:

Employees' views of the competence of top management have turned sharply negative. Noting that all employee groups, including managers, have lowered ratings of top management since the late 1970's, ORC says that the decline "is very pronounced and widespread, and is one symptom of top management's becoming more isolated from employees and less responsive to employees' concerns."[5]

Noting how the survey findings impact productivity and operating effectiveness, the researchers concluded that:

ORC findings indicate that employees' general lack of confidence in top management is translated into specific perceived problems. These include: lack of adequate training; poor cooperation between departments to avoid duplication; poor design of work to minimize destructive stress; and an increasing willingness to keep ineffective workers on the payroll.

All employee groups give their companies generally poor marks for communications, although this is the essence of management. In the mid-1970's employees' assessment of communications was trending upward. Now more employees feel that the company doesn't keep them informed enough about what's going on. *Increasingly, employees—especially hourly—question what their companies do tell them.*

Companies rate no better in upward communication—being willing to listen to employees on problems and suggestions.

Finally, all employee groups say that the company grapevine is their first source of information. They don't prefer it that way—they would like to get information from supervisors—*face to face.* . . .

The message is clear: top management must reestablish its ties with employees in order to better solve productivity problems and meet employee needs.[6] (Emphasis added.)

What does this research show?

First, it provides evidence in support of the claim that how the people at the top are viewed by employees throughout the organization is a critical ingredient—perhaps the most critical—of a satisfying work experience.

Second, it tells us that we ought to be paying much more attention to the critical communication linkage between top management and the rest of the organization. The relationship between employees and the supervisory level of management remains just as important as it has always been, but now we know there is another, even more influential relationship between top management and employees.

Third, it gives us compelling reasons to take action—to do something about improving employee views of the top and thereby improve work attitudes, which we believe are the triggering key ingredients of a chain of action needed for a renaissance in American corporate leadership.

The why and how of such actions are the reasons for this book.

The best approach to a genuine dialogue with employees is through their perception of top management. This concept must be taken to heart and acted upon conscientiously by U.S. corporate leaders lest the gap between American productivity and that of our international competitors widen even more dangerously.

America's chief executives must learn how to handle their power as a positive influence on employee attitudes. They possess a natural force for improving worker attitudes, but they must learn how to take advantage of this genuine opportunity to boost overall corporate effectiveness. The critical role of the CEO is the essential new dimension of corporate leadership that must be brought into play if American business is to regain its true place in the world order of industrial influence.

There must be a different geopolitical dynamic working internationally in the world of business to enable America's corporate leadership to initiate the new industrial renaissance from which all in the United States can draw benefits. And we believe that in the traditional spirit of America's willingness to share its expertise, this industrial self-renewal is destined to enrich other nations' industrial communities as well. It is not viewed by us selfishly as an ethocentric nationalistic movement.

We are describing a new managerial revolution in corporate communication. It must be gutsy, honest, and truthful. If it is to be productive in the increasingly severe economic turbulence America faces in the coming decade, it also must follow a new code of business behavior backed up by renewed belief in the importance of the American worker.

A fine example of the kind of communicator we are talking about is Lee A. Iacocca. Examine the way he has steered Chrysler through the rocky shoals of near bankruptcy. He maneuvered, manipulated and employed a combination of frontpage media skills, power politics, and method school of acting techniques to push legislation through Congress to save beleaguered Chrysler from dismemberment.

Now that is outstanding communications skill at work. The professional investment community has been wooed skillfully to provide the cooperation necessary to save and rebuild Chrysler. Iacocca's successful performance in selling the Chrysler refinancing package in the face of what the smart money men in Wall Street saw as insurmountable obstacles is worthy of study. Iacocca and his Chrysler colleagues applied modern communications techniques so adroitly that they achieved a financial rescue package that made business history—a $1.2 billion U.S. Treasury raid to save the third largest U.S. auto maker. That takes immense communication skill and well illustrates the new breed of executive/communicator at work.

That superior communications skill is not confined to the man at the top alone. Those genuinely gifted in the art of communication as a mainstay of executive leadership tend to associate themselves with other executives who are similarly adroit. Or, they train and cultivate their close associates in senior management to become adept communicators. In the case of Chrysler's Iacocca, he brought into the company Robert S. Miller, Jr., when the corporation was facing its darkest hours in 1979. Miller, who was recruited from Ford, is now executive vice president and chief financial officer. He is anything but the conventional stereotype of a sober-sided, grey-pin striped number cruncher.

He has jokingly referred in public to Chrysler's bankers as "a bunch of turkeys." Once when negotiating with the jittery lenders he pulled a toy pistol, pointed it at his head and threatened to shoot unless they agreed to a Chrysler proposal. During one particularly difficult session, an executive of one of Chrysler's foreign banks recalls, Miller offered a proposal: "How about a compromise? You agree to what I want and I'll agree to stop calling you names."[7]

That is one good example of tactical communications at work. Miller has all the proper credentials—a Harvard law degree and a Stanford MBA—plus an innate understanding of the need to communicate in a new way when the chips are down. Did it work? Let the record show that Miller came away from these negotiating sessions with a surprising agreement that in effect wiped $1.2 billion in debt off Chrysler's books.

To be effective at this level of expertise in corporate communication requires that men and women at the top to commit themselves to a new order of thinking. In the executive suite of tomorrow these leaders must be communicators extraordinaire. This collective and multifaceted new role for CEOs will be key in restoring the luster to America's new industrial commanders of the economy into the twenty-first century.

In the new international environment of business leadership, facing up to ever increasing world competition is going to take a generation of American business leaders schooled not so much in Reaganomics as in Ronald Reagan's mastery of the communication arts.

CHAPTER 3

The Renaissance in Corporate Leadership

Genius, in truth, means little more than the faculty of perceiving in an unhabitual way.

William James

THE TERM "Renaissance man" calls to mind a person of broad intellectual interests encompassing a full spectrum of available knowledge and wisdom. From the fourteenth through the seventeenth century, Europe experienced the Renaissance, a time of great intellectual and artistic revival during which the creative spirit was given free rein. Truly, the Renaissance represented a time of renewal for the human spirit unique in history. American business and industry today yearn for this kind of new dawning, and that is why we have chosen the word "renaissance" to describe our call for new leadership to emerge.

In America today our corporations, our society, and our government need a new quality of leadership and the honesty, directness, and truthfulness in communication that are its prime ingredients.

The ethical practice of communication in business can be the least costly common denominator in regaining lost markets, reinspiring the workforce, and rebuilding the public's dwindling faith in American industry. We believe the renaissance in American corporate leadership must be solidly based on the principles of good communication. Of all the forces and conditions that influence the course of business leadership, communication is the one thread that can make the difference. It is time now to rearticulate the power that leaders of any organization hold through the means and methods of human communication over which they have enormous influence.

The corporate leaders we are seeking to develop are today a tiny minority. They represent perhaps less than 1 percent of the corporate leadership in the United States. How better to describe the combination of artistic, intellectual and emotional qualities that make up this kind of unique and influential leader than through the word "renaissance"?

The formula is simple: American corporate leadership is clearly in a state of crisis. Communication is, we believe, the pathway out of this crisis, and top management is the focal point for the effort.

CEOs' Sixth Sense

There is a sixth sense that some corporate leaders have that qualifies them for positions in a corporate Communication Hall of Fame. They have not learned their communication skills in business school, or even by majoring in English or linguistics or taking an advanced degree in sociology or divinity. Rather, the skills these top-rated business executives possess in communication spring from abilities that make them good leaders in the first instance: a combination of good instincts and a keen sensitivity to what works. They cultivate people-oriented behavior in themselves. Their caring about others shows and it is genuine. No Madison Avenue or public relations type ever had to tell these leaders how to behave. Untruthfulness in advertising or any form of communication isn't countenanced.

Just as the Founding Fathers of the Republic knew that freedom of information and the truthful sharing of the facts were cornerstones of American democracy as expressed in the Constitution, so too renaissance leaders of business accept the premise that truth telling is basic to sound business. They know that workers, customers, suppliers, and government agencies all must have open access to honest facts. Ethical behavior and morality in business philosophies are living guidelines that shape the spirit and actions of companies on whose leaders, employees, and products the consumer can count.

"Public relations," in its classic sense, has a breadth, a scope and harmony with society's highest purposes that we feel most executives and leaders could comfortably accept.

The definition we prefer is this:

Public relations is the management function that evaluates public attitudes, identifies the policies and procedures of an individual or an organization with the public interest, and executes a program of action to earn public understanding and acceptance.

For decades, PR types have been sulking and wringing their hands over the fact that they have not yet been accorded a place at the conference table of senior management. Louis B. Lundborg, when he was chairman of Bank of America, dissected the issue of how management looks at public relations:

> For members of management *are* public relations oriented in the truest sense of the term. They have to be, for their jobs—effectively running a business—require that they consider every so-called public sector that exists in relationship to the whole company and its goals. Management must necessarily gauge each act of the corporation within this total perspective. If the public relations men will make the necessary effort and commitment to achieve this same perspective—and it requires a lot of work to learn intimately the total thrust of a concern—then a place at the management conference table will be willingly, even eagerly, accorded.
>
> Conversely, if public relations remains trapped by its own specific perspective then it will be relegated to the status of a technical department. This brings me to the final myth—that "good communications will solve every problem." In point of fact, this is simply not true. In the first place, it is an unfortunate condition of life that not every so-called problem has a solution. Furthermore many of the problems that do admit of solution require the application of a lot more than the vaunted communication skills—polished and effective as they may be.
>
> The hard and simple fact is that in a changing world the most brilliantly effective communication of an outdated shibboleth will avail nothing. "What" is communicated is as vital—more vital—than "how."[1]

Far too many slick word artists from the world of Madison Avenue try to cross over into the executive halls of business leadership and find it hard to shed the ways of double-speak. Pushing to erect a screen of images to obscure poor products, nondescript no-service, and business conduct that hovers near illegality or, at best, follows the quick-buck routine, such manipulators have done irreparable damage to the image of a noble group—the truth tellers. This is what Louis Lundborg was decrying in urging the demise of outdated shibboleths and worship of the medium to the detriment of the message.

Thomas J. Watson, Jr., when he was president of giant IBM, was not reluctant to acknowledge that the single most important factor in the business success of his company was its commitment to good public relations, which stemmed from his father's instincts and genius in that area. He recalls with fondness his father's sensitive "feel" for the importance of the right name for the fledgling company in 1923 when he chose "International Business Machines Corporation."

> He came home one evening . . . and announced that he was changing the name of the Company from the Computing, Tabulating and Recording Company to the International Business Machines Corporation.
>
> I thought that this was a pretty big name for something that didn't impress me very much. But the name itself was another indication of the early public relations consciousness of the Corporation which was being carried out by our "Director of Public Relations"—who carried the title of President.
>
> Father always talked and acted as though IBM were a billion dollar corporation, even in the twenties, even though the income was less than 2% of the volume we have now reached. By this continued positive, aggressive thinking, he was able to lift the Corporation by its bootstraps for a tremendous distance.
>
> He was the master of grand gesture. At the New York Worlds Fair of 1939, there was a General Motors Day, a General Electric and an IBM day . . . two elephants and a gnat all getting the same treatment. We even had Mayor LaGuardia as our guest at the Fair that day.
>
> Further, he brought every employee of our then only factory down to the Worlds Fair on a visit . . . this on 20 special trains from Endicott to New York.
>
> On the way back, one of the trains was wrecked. Dad was 66 years old, but he got up in the middle of the night . . . drove to the hospital and greeted every employee hurt in the wreck and then endowed the hospital generously for their help to IBM.
>
> Dad's handling of the wreck is still a legend and a goal for us all in IBM.[2]

This instinct to sense the mood, timing, and importance of a situation and then unerringly take the right action and say the right thing the right way, with sensitive consideration to how people will react to the company's behavior, is the stuff of which effective communication is made. From that ability flows the creative energy to make an ordinary company great.

Yet some CEOs have a well-developed capacity to say the wrong thing at the wrong time in the wrong way. Who can forget the arrogance of "Engine Charlie" Wilson telling Congress that "what's good for General Motors is good for the nation"? Commodore Vanderbilt's classic remark "The public be damned" will live in business history as one the communications blunders of all time.

Bad communication can also be the product of insensitivity to timing. Beleagured International Harvester, fighting for survival, implored the UAW to grant wage and benefit concessions that would lower its cost of doing business by $200 million in the winter recession of 1981. In the same week that the union grudgingly agreed to yield on those issues so dear to the hearts of the labor union leaders who had to please *their* constituents, Harvester's management announced the award of a new and liberalized management incentive compensation plan that would cost $6 million! Little wonder the UAW went to the media the next day steaming and fuming at being "taken" and "used."

And while we are analyzing goofs of timing in relationship to sound use of the communication process, we cannot overlook General Motors. "Dumbest Move of the Year" read the local Detroit columnist's account of GM's handling of its new accord with the UAW in the spring of 1982.

The renegotiated GM contract provided for extensive union concessions and signaled, both parties had hoped, the start of a new and more cordial atmosphere between management and its workers.[3] An elaborate breakfast was organized to celebrate the new pact. Labor, management, and the press were to join in the happy occasion. But at 4 P.M. on the very day of the media event, General Motors issued its proxy statement for the upcoming annual meeting. In it was disclosed a new program of a sweetened bonus package for its top executives, plus a new incentive formula and an extended stock option plan. New riches for the bosses; for the workers, more sacrifices for the good of the company. GM's blue-collar workers protested that they had been tricked; white-collar workers also felt used. The possibility of a strike caused GM to announce that the new benefit plans wouldn't be used.

GM Chairman Roger B. Smith publicly admitted he was startled at the outcry. "I was surprised at the intensity of the reaction," he said. Douglas Fraser, president of the United Auto Workers, said "I've never seen a situation where the workers were more upset." At Pontiac, Michigan, Ted Creason, bargaining chairman at UAW Local 653, exclaimed, "It may be quite some time before we gain back the confidence the workers had just two weeks ago. The atmosphere is total mistrust."

So explosive was the environment that the workers blamed Roger Smith personally, and the key adjective they used was "arrogant."

As in all catastrophes, after the event Roger Smith was musing to himself, as reported in the *Wall Street Journal* on April 13, 1982, "I'm impatient, but I don't think I'm arrogant." He acknowledged that "a whole bunch of us" in GM management knew that the austere contract and the extended bonuses were coming simultaneously. "Was there anybody who came out and said that the union was going to react violently to this? I don't remember anyone saying that."

Yet General Motors has one of the biggest and most expensive systems for internal and external communication in industry. Over 50 GM communications professionals are members of the Public Relations Society of America. Organizationally, it has five professional communicators in GM Internal Communications at the corporate level. "Each of 140 GM locations has a person designated as internal communications coordinator. In addition, we have about 160 editors producing a variety of employee publications throughout GM."[4] Thus about 305 people at GM are paid to concentrate on employee communication, although it is true that many work only part time.

In 1982 GM spent $2.7 billion on selling and administrative expenses, which include all forms of corporate communication. Yet, the chairman says, no one spoke up. Why not?

To give you an idea of how far General Motors has strayed from its original mission as renaissance communicator, we have to go back to the genius of Alfred P. Sloan, Jr. This pioneering builder of the modern business management system of GM, who led the corporation for 23 years as CEO, had an instinct for the use of public relations as communication that was rare. He knew that without public permission there could be no profitable General Motors.

> According to my philosophy, the purpose of public relations is twofold. First, recognizing that most our economy is in large-scale, privately owned enterprises, I think the first, but perhaps not foremost, responsi-

bility of public relations is to give full information to the public and to its own shareholders concerning what's going on in the business so far as can properly be disclosed. The second phase is, I think, for public relations to explore the relationship of the enterprise to its social responsibility. . . . You should tell what the enterprise does, how it does it in relation to its social responsibility, and especially the importance of maintaining what we call in this country the free enterprise system.[5]

Rudderless Corporate Communication

Our experience is that even in many of the biggest and presumably the most advanced companies in America, the communication function remains fragmented and disjointed. The organization chart may point up that there is someone in command of communication, but in reality, unending sorry events of the past years show that most often the corporate ship is rudderless in this vital business area when it hits stormy seas.

At Three Mile Island, General Public Utilities had no communication emergency plan. It took the Governor of Pennsylvania, Richard L. Thornburgh, personally to assume calm leadership in the tragic void left by GPU managers, who were too befuddled to inform and reassure a justly worried populace living around Three Mile Island. Add to that the fact that the Nuclear Regulatory Commission was later shown to be saddled with inadequate, sketchy procedures for handling the informational functions of a genuine nuclear emergency. Now you have a fair approximation of business's inability to cope when the chips are down.

In the communications business, any working newsman knows that when things go wrong, everyone clams up. At the very time the public needs information for its own protection, the captains of industry yield to the lawyers and say nothing. Or they start denying truth hoping to be believed.

Stories of ineptitude in the business of disseminating information from corporate America to the public are numerous. Here are a few mistakes with a "10" rating:

Firestone-Walling It

In 1978 a new euphemism for corporate noncommunication entered the language: "Firestone-walling it." This is the label Congressional staffers in Washington coined to describe the roadblocks and obstacles to the truth set up by the Firestone Tire & Rubber Company in the now infamous case of the "500" radial-tire recall.

Consumer complaints were coming in increasing numbers to the National Highway Traffic Safety Administration that Firestone "500" radial tires were blowing out, were not round, and were found to suffer from tread separation. Joan Claybrook, the federal agency's administrator and a former consumer activist, initiated a survey among radial-tire owners to check on the accuracy of the complaints. Of 2,226 responses from Firestone "500" tire users, 46 percent reported tire problems. This was substantially higher than problems reported by owners of other brands of radial tires. Other makers were found to have a report of problems at 33 percent for Goodrich radials, 32 percent for Goodyear and Uniroyal, 26 percent for General Tire, and only 2 percent for Michelin.

Claybrook's agency analysts calculated that the 784 consumer reports of Firestone radial-tire failures represented 8.8 percent of each 1,000 new radial tires sold by Firestone for the 1975 to 1977 model years. This compared with only 2.35 percent for Goodrich, the next highest tire failure rating.

The *Akron Beacon-Journal* in July reported that Firestone discovered serious problems with its "500" tires in 1975.[6] A computer printout of test results from tires in warehouse stock awaiting shipment to General Motors showed that 56.5 percent of the tires failed to meet a critical government high-speed performance standard. Firestone management released a statement in response to the newspaper story that contended its tires were safe and reliable and discounted the significance of its own computer test results.

Instead of assuming responsibility for the product defects and acting to protect the public and its customers, Firestone's leaders apparently began to listen to the company's lawyers and not its professional communications staff. They decided to lay the blame on the tire owners themselves, saying they mishandled the tires and thus they blew out. The National Highway Traffic Safety Administration then reported that the "500" had been involved in 14,000 tire failures, 29 deaths and 50 injuries, and hundreds of accidents which contributed to property damage.

Firestone-walling continued as management ordered its communications people to put out denials. The *New York Times* on July 8, 1978, quoted a Firestone spokesman, "The '500' is providing reliable service to millions of motorists today as it has for many years. There is no safety-related reason for the public to be concerned about continuing to use Firestone steel-belted radial 500s or any other properly maintained Firestone-made tire." Finally, in October 1978, Firestone agreed with the government to recall about 10 million "500s" while steadfastly maintaining that the tires had no safety defects. Management set up a reserve of $200 million to cover the cost of the recall. The company subsequently established a $3 million settlement fund to help satisfy purchasers of the tires.

"Firestone's actions in this case give American industry a black eye," Claybrook said. "This is an example of a company that was knowledgeable of the problem for a long time and attempted to divert the agency from an investigation."[7] She then announced that she was planning to fine Firestone $800,000. On December 2, 1978, the *Washington Post* stated in an editorial, "Certainly sanctions are in order. Firestone should have moved a lot faster on a serious safety matter."

If anyone wants a classic example of how the communication function can be prostituted to stress the Big Lie, we nominate this one.

However, in the interest of fairness and recognizing that what is on the public record in media coverage can sometimes be erroneous, we contacted Firestone management and asked it to comment on the Firestone "500" confrontation from the perspective of five years of contemplation after the fact. This is part of their response:

> There is no question but that Firestone's image was harmed by the way we handled the Firestone "500" situation. There is also no question that, given the advantage of hindsight, we might have handled some aspect of it differently. And if we had done things differently, we might have avoided some of the misleading or incomplete information that appeared in the press. . . .
>
> In the case of the NHTSA survey, for example, the NHTSA official who designed and conducted it, Lynn Bradford, admitted in a sworn deposition that it "was not a survey designed to yield results having any statistical significance. . . ."
>
> Also relevant to an understanding of the "500" situation is the information in the enclosed SAE technical paper by Failure Analysis Associates, which is an engineering firm specializing in accident reconstruction and risk quantification. This company, at the request of Firestone, undertook an evaluation of the safety record of the Firestone "500.". . .
>
> The Failure Analysis Associates study compared tire related accident rates of vehicles equipped with Firestone's *recalled* steel belted

radial tires with rates experienced by the same vehicles equipped with all other original equipment manufacturers' tires. . . .

> The conclusion of the study. . . .
> "In sum . . . Firestone's recalled '500' tire proved safer than the average of all other original equipment manufacturers' tires combined in the largest tire accident survey ever conducted."

. . . there are two sides to the story and . . . Firestone acted with integrity in what was a very difficult and extremely complex matter which is much simpler to address in hindsight than it was at the time it was taking place.[8]

Now the federal government has spoken, the press has spoken, and here Firestone's executive leadership has expressed its views and fresh facts. We repeat, there is a better way to handle such product failure issues. Openness, complete candor, and acting swiftly to be on the side of the public interest seem clearly the way to behave.

Ford Pinto

Triggered by an article, "Pinto Madness," that appeared in the September–October 1977 issue of *Mother Jones,* the media jumped on the story of burn deaths and injuries from Pinto rear-end collisions. The original charge was that Ford Motor Company had rushed pre-1977 Ford Pintos into production while knowing of a defect in the gas tank. The tank, made of thin-gauge steel, was located too near the rear bumper and was easily punctured in rear-end crashes at 20 mph or more. This article claimed 500 to 900 burn deaths resulted over a six-year period.

In May 1978, the Department of Transportation's National Highway Traffic Safety Administration announced that its investigation had found fuel-tank defects in 1.9 million Ford Pintos and in 30,000 Mercury Bobcats that presented an unreasonable risk to safety. Reacting to the public pressure, Ford recalled the cars and offered to make modifications in a voluntary recall.

In an Elkhart, Indiana, trial over the burn deaths of three teenage girls in a flaming Pinto, Henry Ford II and then Ford President Lee A. Iacocca were issued summonses to testify about the Pinto fuel-tank design. But the two top Ford executives were never drawn into the court procedure. An Indiana jury acquitted the Ford Motor

Company of reckless homicide after a 10-week trial. Other civil suits were then settled out of court.

We asked Ford Motor Company what its management had learned from the Pinto incident and what advice its management could give other CEOs from this experience. Walter Hayes, vice president for public affairs, wrote to us through an associate:

> It is very difficult to relate past events to what is going on today because times have changed, people have changed and experience has characterized past events and essentially changed them. For example, Ford Motor Company isn't the same company today in many essential respects that it was during the Pinto matter.
>
> There are several points that should be made in connection with the Pinto:
>
> —It is safe to say that all statements, actions and events will be misunderstood, distorted or ignored by somebody.
>
> —If you are an expert on any subject (and can therefore be considered a good judge), you will discover that any reporter dealing with that subject will invariably get something wrong.
>
> —The average American has to absorb quite complicated facts and issues in one minute and thirty seconds because that, for the most part, is all that television permits him to do.
>
> —This inevitably leads to massive over-simplification of all things.
>
> —Plaintiff attorneys, pressure groups and power seekers who want their bandwagons to catch fire have a vested interest in distortion.
>
> —Despite the publicity, the Pinto continued to sell extraordinarily well.
>
> —Dealers sold cars to their friends and company executives bought them for their children which they would scarely have done if the car had been an accident waiting to happen.
>
> —Many other cars followed the same design principles.
>
> However, . . . a company or organization or individual should recognize these things and understand them and should therefore take every step possible *not to be misunderstood.* This is subtly different from being understood, but it ought to be the key for all communication.
>
> Ford did not change character during the Pinto affair. It has always been a spectacularly open and truthful company and Henry Ford II's personal example over the many years he was at the helm is beyond criticism.
>
> What the Pinto affair did was to underscore the need to go to extraordinary lengths to communicate some not very extraordinary facts.
>
> If there is a lesson that has been learned I suppose this is it, but

I would not say we had learned it as a result of Pinto. It has always been an obvious maxim in communications.[9]

Procter & Gamble as Role Model

There is a better way to handle these product safety problems using good communication as part of a leadership strategy at the top that demonstrates the company genuinely cares about its customers, its reputation, and its responsibility to the public and the community. Just ask Edward G. Harness, the chairman of Procter & Gamble, the venerable and skilled marketer of soaps and other home products in Cincinnati.

When "Rely" brand tampons were found to be a suspected causal factor in toxic shock syndrome deaths by the Federal Center for Disease Control in Atlanta, he ordered the product off the market voluntarily. He organized an emergency task force of seasoned managers on his staff to contain and cope with this problem, and kept the rest of the company's managers free to concentrate on running the rest of the business to its usual high standards of integrity. That decision cost P & G $75 million after taxes, and the episode was fraught with legal implications and trial exposure that will endure for years, but Harness didn't cave in to the lawyers and clam up. Management's behavior in the Rely tampon episode will go down in business annals as an example of a responsible company whose leaders naturally and instinctively put the welfare of the customer above the interests of the corporation—unhesitatingly.

For P & G the stakes were high. It had labored for 20 years with research and marketing preparations to bring Rely tampons into national distribution. It reached full distribution in February 1980, and security analysts estimate that in its first full year Rely would have accounted for $45 million in sales. It garnered an impressive 24 percent of the tampon market in a short time, and industry analysts agreed that it had the momentum to overtake the industry leader, Tampax. Rely was only the first of a family of P & G products. Management had other related products close to readiness for marketing, including a minipad and deodorant tampon, and it was also planning to put the original product into foreign distribution. It was poised to carve out a major portion of an estimated $1 billion feminine protection market.

Management at P & G first became aware of toxic shock in

May 1980, when the Center for Disease Control published findings that many new cases of the syndrome had been documented among menstruating women. In June, P & G was asked for information on its tampon, as were other manufacturers. The CDC continued to study cases of toxic shock contracted in July and found that more than twice as many women afflicted with the disease had used Rely when compared with a similar group of healthy women. This startling research finding was released in mid-September and within a few days was confirmed by another study at the Utah Health Department. Rely was then in grave trouble.

Bad publicity against Rely was being fomented by the Food and Drug Administration, the regulatory agency charged with responsibility to act on the CDC studies. Use of the press by the FDA was part of a planned offensive strategy to drive Rely off the market. Wayne L. Pines, associate FDA commissioner for public affairs, said:

> We wanted to saturate the market with information on Rely. We deliberately delayed issuing press releases for a day to maximize the media impact. There was quite a concerned and deliberate effort to keep a steady flow of information before the public.[10]

The FDA was counting on P & G's sensitivity to bad publicity about any of its products as well as the company's natural concern about its own responsibility to protect public health.

Though Procter & Gamble had never before in its 143-year history faced a crisis decision of this magnitude, Chairman Harness and his senior officers made the decision within a week to withdraw Rely from the market. It eventually took 3,000 P & G employees to pull the product out of stores and physically to remove it from the channels of distribution nationwide.

In reflecting on that momentous decision, Mr. Harness says, "We did the right thing in suspending the brand. I don't think we could have moved any sooner than we did because we couldn't get any data. And we couldn't have moved any slower or else we would have gotten into a bloodbath of wholly negative publicity." His advice for other CEOs who may have to face similar disaster decisions: "Keep the ball in your own court, if you can. Do it right before somebody else does it wrong for you."[11] That's $75 million worth of advice from a corporate leader who has been through the test of fire.

In his personal report to the shareholders of P & G at the

annual meeting on October 14, 1980, Mr. Harness told the assembled owners of the company, "We believe we have done what is right and that our action is consistent with the long-held Procter & Gamble view that the Company alone is responsible for the safety of our products. To sacrifice this principle could over the years ahead be a far greater cost than the monetary losses we face on the Rely brand."[12]

Johnson & Johnson's Brilliance

It is ironic that sometimes tragedy must strike to demonstrate the inherent quality and responsible business leadership that sustains the growth and profitability of some of America's most respected corporations.

Certainly Johnson & Johnson and its corporate behavior in the face of seven deaths from cyanide-laced Extra Strength Tylenol capsules present a business role model worthy of emulating. In contrast to the evasiveness of Firestone's and Ford's management behavior, one need only review the highlights of the actions taken swiftly and surely by Johnson & Johnson when tragedy hit its leading consumer product line to discern the thought patterns of executive leadership at the top which acted to protect consumers and the public safety—at any cost. Humane and compassionate communication lay at the center of the business leadership exhibited by James E. Burke, Johnson & Johnson's chairman and chief executive officer, in the whole Tylenol episode.

The bizarre and macabre story began at 9:30 A.M. Thursday, September 30, 1982, when James Burke first heard that three persons in the Chicago area had died after taking Tylenol capsules. Authorities found that the country's most successful over-the-counter pain reliever had been laced with lethal doses of cyanide.

Tylenol is produced by J & J's McNeil Consumer Products Company, headquartered in Fort Washington, Pennsylvania. About a hundred million Americans are known to have taken the analgesic last year. Tylenol sales were expected to reach $500 million in 1983. In 1981 it had 37 percent of the $1.5 billion analgesic market, contributed 8 percent of J & J's worldwide sales of $5.4 billion, and analysts estimated that it contributed about 14 to 19 percent of the corporation's earnings of $467.6 million in 1981. J & J's brilliant positioning strategy had made marketing history, and in the past few years it had far outdistanced its main competitor. It was a wonder product in every classic dimension of modern marketing. But now its product life was threatened by an unprecedented, eerie attack on its purpose. From a pain reliever, it had overnight become a deadly killer.

Within days the death toll rose to seven, all from the Chicago area. The most shattering emotional burden seemed to focus on the funeral of 12-year-old Mary Kellerman. Many J & J employees wept when they saw on TV the small casket crowned with flowers.

The Tylenol murders were front-page news all over the nation. In New York alone, the TV stations ran over 21 solid hours of Tylenol-related news in the early weeks of the tragedy. J & J's Corporate Public Relations Department has accumulated nearly 120,000 news stories on the grim mystery. Lawrence G. Foster, J & J's seasoned corporate vice president of public relations, and his staff fielded 2,500 phone calls from the media seeking further information as the story continued to be top news for many weeks.

From the very moment the disaster struck, J & J reacted with openness, honesty, and candor that has won the company and its management praise from press and public alike. McNeil Consumer Products uses cyanide in a testing procedure for ingredients. This was readily acknowledged by Foster in his working contacts with the press, when he explained that it was only a small quantity in a separate laboratory, not a part of the manufacturing process. Investigation of the manufacturing system proved that the high levels of the poison found in the victims' blood would have required massive quantities of cyanide in the batch process. This key fact and the built-in safeguards for product purity in the factory process were made public in the totally open communication system Burke and Foster used throughout the episode. As a result, the credibility of the corporation was never in question. The media have been uncharacteristically demonstrative in acknowledging the professionalism and honesty they found in their dealings with J & J.

Management cooperated fully with the press and worked immediately with the Food and Drug Administration as well as the FBI and the local law enforcement agencies in Chicago and Cook County, Illinois, to utilize all of its business resources to aid the massive manhunt for the murderer.

As the world knows, J & J voluntarily initiated a massive recall of 31 million bottles of Extra Strength Tylenol. Burke flew to Washington and personally met with Dr. Arthur Hayes, Jr., commissioner of the FDA, and also met with FBI Director William Webster to jointly work out plans to effect the recall and to make it impossible for the tragedy to stimulate copy-cat crimes.

Burke called a meeting of 50 J & J company presidents and corporate staffers on Tuesday morning, October 12, and they made an "unequivocal decision" to put the full resources of Johnson & Johnson behind the recall effort, to support and cooperate by lending extra hands and organization to McNeil Consumer Products because the international reputation of Johnson & Johnson itself was at stake.

Management made the important decision to retain the name Tylenol and not try to re-market it under another name, as several experts had suggested. J & J's marketing and sales executives had begun the arduous task of determining how to rebuild the product reputation. Tylenol was going to stand on its own reputation, and already plans were under way to develop a new system of tamper-resistant packaging.

A corporate strategy group of seven senior executives was formed by James Burke and included David R. Clare, president of J & J and chairman of its Executive Committee and corporate communications officer Lawrence Foster. At McNeil different teams dealt with the complex problems of resurrecting the Tylenol business and quickly designing tamper-resistant packaging methods. Burke himself headed the tamper-resistant packaging team. All knew that the key to saving the product line was to evolve a foolproof new packaging barrier and get it into the marketplace under emergency power.

High drama charged many of the J & J team efforts to scour the world for packaging and engineering machinery and know-how to develop a new tamper-resistant packaging system that would thwart any adulteration of Tylenol on store shelves. On Thursday, November 4, Burke personally demonstrated a new packaging system in Washington to Dr. Hayes, the FDA commissioner, and to Richard Schweiker, Secretary of Health and Human Services. J & J had devised a triple system of barriers to protect the capsules. Schweiker was pleased. He called it an "armored tank."

A week later, Burke introduced the new packaging to the nation in a unique 30-city closed-circuit television press conference beamed from New York via satellite. In four cities—Chicago, Philadelphia, Washington, and Los Angeles—reporters had a two-way audio hookup enabling them to question Burke and other company officers about the new marketing plan and the new packaging, and the policy of direct, honest communication continued.

Burke reported that J & J was spending $100 million on the Tylenol recall and was going to absorb the full cost of the new tamper-resistant packaging system.

The next day, November 12, James Burke flew to San Diego to address the annual conference of the Associated Press Managing Editors. He reviewed the Tylenol story for the assembled influential editors.

> Eight million capsules have been tested by us and the authorities. Seventy-five Tylenol capsules laced with cyanide were found. Eight bottles had been tampered with. But an important note, two of those bottles were found as a result of our recall so perhaps our mutual efforts in fact did save some lives. . . .
>
> Thirty-five percent of all Tylenol users threw away the product because of the fear that was generated. Eighty percent of all people who were not regular Tylenol users say they will never consider using Tylenol. Forty-one percent of regular Tylenol users are not sure they will use the product again. . . .
>
> While 41 percent of our users said they might not use Tylenol again, the flip side of that is very positive in the face of the story that has been told. Fifty-nine percent of our Tylenol users said they would repurchase Tylenol and 77 percent said they would if we put it in a tamper resistant container.
>
> Finally, we have offered to replace the Tylenol free of charge that our consumers threw away. We are very optimistic about the future of Tylenol.[13]

How has the media reacted to Burke's candor and the massive impact of open communication at full throttle? The *Washington Post* said:

> Johnson and Johnson has effectively demonstrated how a major business ought to handle a disaster.
>
> This is no Three Mile Island accident in which the company's response did more damage than the original incident. There has been no Nixonian "modified limited hangout" at the J & J headquarters in New Brunswick, N.J.
>
> No one at the McNeil Consumer Products subsidiary has tried to pretend that nothing is wrong, as Firestone Tire and Rubber Co. officials did when the Firestone 500 tires were disintegrating.
>
> Nor has the company yielded to the temptation to pillory the media, not even when sensation-seekers tried to link a suicide in Philadelphia in April to the murders in Chicago last week. Not even the

publicity-grabbing Chicago prosecutor—who just happened to be running for higher office—has been able to prompt a backlash from the company.

What J & J executives have done is communicate the message that the company is candid, contrite and compassionate, committed to solving the murders and protecting the public.[14]

In terms of the marketing prowess that originally won the lion's share of the over-the-counter analgesic market, has J & J made the right moves to regain its leadership position?

Stephen E. Permut, a marketing professor at Yale University who studies product recalls and consumer product safety, has said of Tylenol's preempting the competition by being first to announce— in a nationally reported press conference rather than a TV ad— new triple-layer tamper-resistant packaging:

> That was brilliant. Tylenol becomes the standard to which every other brand is compared. The others will just be making a "me too" kind of claim.[15]

James Burke, every inch the renaissance business executive, went on the Phil Donahue Show and for 47 minutes answered questions and responded to consumers' queries and natural interest in probing how the CEO felt about and reacted to the Tylenol episode.

Burke, whom his associates admiringly describe as "a marketing animal"[16] with an uncanny knack for dead-reckoning consumer psychology, unhesitatingly emphasized that the company never had any second thoughts about not absorbing all the costs in the recall and the development of the new tamper-resistant packaging. He also emphasized that Johnson & Johnson had a moral responsibility to protect its customers and the medical profession.

He reminded the public that J & J has a corporate credo, conceived and written in 1944 by Robert Wood Johnson, son of the founder of the company and its chairman for 31 years. The first sentence of the credo says, "We believe our first responsibility is to the doctors, nurses and patients, to mothers and all others who use our products and services." Burke made it clear that J & J takes that business philosophy seriously and that it was a source of strength to refer to those words when weighing and evaluating the costly moves that had to be made. He got a rousing round of applause from the studio audience. One woman lauded him for showing such admirable "social responsibility."

Joseph R. Chiesa, president, McNeil Consumer Products, told

Fortune magazine, "The problem with consumer research is that it reflects attitudes and not behavior. The best way to know what the consumers are going to do is put the product back on the shelves and let them vote with their hands."[17]

A McNeil Company survey of physicians and pharmacists has shown solid evidence of strong support for the product and continued usage and recommendations. Eighty-four percent of primary-care physicians surveyed indicated they would recommend Tylenol capsules in tamper-resistant packaging. Ninety-two percent of all pharmacists who had used the product previously said they would use it again.[18]

But doing it right for Johnson & Johnson under the leadership of James Burke didn't develop overnight; it followed in the well-worn tracks of a company committed to being in the "people business." A talk with Burke personally to learn what his innermost thoughts were during those terrible days of the Tylenol murder crisis revealed that he is disarmingly candid, open, and very human about his feelings:

A business, to be successful over the long term, has to be responsive to all of its constituencies. This is true of all institutions, but I believe businesses are often better disciplined to be responsive. If they are not . . . they go out of business. I think we have to be more responsive than other institutions, or we are going to go out of business.

Our task as managers is to maintain a structure of organization that will encourage and make possible the responsiveness that is at the heart of our existence. One of our great strengths as a company is that we have a set of truths in our credo which helps bring us together, even though we are a big company operating worldwide.

What I quickly saw when the tragedy hit was that we were all in this together. We quickly saw that what started as a business problem for us immediately became a national problem when someone turned a valuable product into a murder weapon. This converted us all to partners dealing with the same problem. Our employees sensed this immediately, but so did the media and the authorities. Everyone was bonded together in a common effort. This was a profound happening.

The first thing we needed to find out was how our customers were feeling and reacting. We sent out teams of people to interview users of Tylenol, and we urged them to articulate their feelings to us. We looked at the numbers, but we also watched and listened to our customers on videotape. But I have grown up in this business talking to people, and the original success of Tylenol was built on the personal touch. It was all very human. It was our field salespeople talking to a doctor about the product. After he prescribed it and saw its success, he talked on his own to someone else. That's how we built that product line into a success over the years.

We are a people-oriented company. We are a family of companies, and most of us have grown up in this family atmosphere. We travel together, we work closely, and we are close to our customers. Those customers know we care about them because we do. My biggest concern as we grow is how to preserve that culture of the family, now that we have nearly 240 locations around the world. About six years ago, Larry Foster set up a video network for us, and we talk to our people through that medium, and they talk to each other with that network.

When we have our employee annual meeting, we all spend months getting ready for that because that opportunity to talk to all of our people is so vital to our future. The energy in this business comes from the bottom up, not top down. They run us, not we them. Our bond to our people is a kind of religion with us. Much of what we do is intuitive, not necessarily quantifiable with numbers. We built Tylenol with intuitive decisions because we were and are close to our customers, and we saved it the same way. These are human decisions.[19]

We nominate this Johnson & Johnson story of responsible corporate leadership as the case example of the decade on how to do it right.

Some companies' images are fixed in the American consumers' conscience as businesses which care about people and go about the task of serving their needs sensibly, at fair prices and with service and quality that keep them coming back for more, decade after decade. When we study these companies of excellence, we find profit performances over the long sweep that are steady, reliable, and consistent with well-defined pathways of predetermined corporate goals.

Sears, Roebuck & Co. is surely one of these winners. IBM is in the same big league, as are Procter & Gamble, AT&T, Deere & Company, Herman Miller, Inc., Texas Instruments, Johnson & Johnson, and others among the brightest and best in American industry.

The Americana of Sears

If Sears, Roebuck and Co. has the greatest retailing franchise in America as expressed in its annual report, it is deserved, even though sales and profits have leveled off in recent years.

There is a special feeling the American consumer has about Sears, and its employees, stockholders, suppliers, the communities it serves, and the nation itself have all benefited from the company founded by Richard Warren Sears. Good communication is so fundamental to Sears' success that its antecedents in the lore of Sears' management philosophies are worth reviewing by today's generation of business managers, or anyone in a leadership position in our society. In education, in political and governmental life, and in the not-for-profit sector, these principles will enrich all who apply them. General Robert E. Wood, the much-loved and much-respected president of Sears, was responsible for a large portion of its growth and setting the tone for the company's behavior as a good business citizen. He expressed many of his innermost feelings about Sears at a company banquet in 1950. We think his words live on today.

> The customer is our real employer. The moment we lose his confidence, that moment marks the beginning of the disintegration of this company. The confidence of the American people in the values, the fairness and the honesty of Sears, Roebuck and Co. is the most precious asset this company has.
>
> The greatest weakness of the modern large corporation is the fact that too often controls and planning are so centralized that the great mass of employees begin to work and give only a small measure of their potential to their work.[20]

He then went on to quote from a 1948 Personnel Department report urging that at all times Sears managers should be alert to:

1. The right of everyone to be treated as an individual and respected as a person.

2. The right of everyone to fairness and justice in all of their relations with colleagues and superiors.

General Wood then stressed to his assembled officers and managers, the heart of the company at that time:

> We must always consider our 150,000 employees as 150,000 individual human beings with personalities of their own. Just as far as humanly possible, our officers, our merchants, our managers, all Sears people in key positions should do everything in their power to allow each and every one of those people under them to have a measure of self-expression, even those in the humblest of jobs. I believe there is no limit to what can be accomplished by a force of employees who are

given an opportunity for self-expression, who have faith in their leaders, who believe not only in their ability, but in their fairness and justice, and who in return give of their best, freely and willingly. If all of Sears is animated by this spirit, nothing can stop us.[21]

Theodore V. Houser, the Sears CEO in a later era, in presenting a lecture at Columbia University in 1957 on "Big Business and Its Publics," articulated the Sears credo on communication to its customers by saying:

In our own approach to our customers, we have taken the position that the more informed they are, the better customers they will be. We have gone to great lengths to keep them informed—through full disclosure of merchandise characteristics in detailed catalog copy, informative labels and so on. We believe in giving customers all the facts about our merchandise so they can make sound decisions.[22]

One of Sears' most expert of communicators, James C. Worthy, the pioneering vice president of public relations, now retired, told Sears executives in a 1958 speech:

The maintenance of a climate of public opinion which is favorable to the operation of a business system requires the maintenance of confidence in the integrity of management. People must be assured, not by words but by deeds, that the system is serving the needs of society at large and not merely of owners and managers. Business must be administered as a public trust, and people's experience with business must give them grounds for believing that this is an operative fact and not a pious platitude.[23]

When we reread the words of these early business executives who built this magnificent merchandising company, we see principles and lessons in wisdom which hold the promise of great tomorrows for thousands of large and small companies today. We urge the present generation of managers to study and apply that wisdom daily in their own businesses and in their personal behavior.

There are common thrusts of unity in philosophy and planning that run through all great companies. All have a common core of devotion to respect for the dignity of the individual and delivering top-quality products and services.

"A family feeling" is the way James Burke at Johnson & Johnson describes the corporate culture. He almost echoes the words and thoughts of another CEO at the top—Donald F. Craib, Jr. a 33-year veteran at Allstate Insurance Company, the Sears wholly owned subsidiary. Craib was a Sears vice chairman before being named to the top post at the huge insurance company with 40,000 employees.

> Judson Branch, when he was chairman of Allstate, talked about our company's emphasis on cooperation and working together as a family of people as a form of "religion." I think there is a great truth in that concept. We do have a company heritage. It is a form of company culture. It is a feeling of belonging. It cultivates a feeling about your work and helps develop a sense of pride. It is a form of *esprit de corps*. It has been built up over the years by all the CEOs who preceded me, and it is part of our heritage which I have to preserve.[24]

Allstate has turned to a company video network to talk to all of its workforce spread nationwide over 22 regions. To take the pulse of what its employees want to talk about and issues that are of concern to them, the company conducts employee attitude studies. From these it sifts down the areas of interest for management to cover. Then it takes a random selection of employees from all levels in the company and brings them together for a group discussion. Those in the group are urged to reflect the questions and concerns of peers from their departments or work areas. That composite group then meets face to face with Craib and President Richard Haayen for several hours, and the open dialogue is videotaped. From that collective footage is edited a 30-minute videotape that is then viewed by employees in headquarters and in the field. Craib reports that the Allstate plan is to talk by video with its people three times a year, a procedure supplemented with a wide range of other printed and oral communications throughout the year.

Analysis of the record shows that the Sears brand of caring is readily transferable to Allstate, and Craib quickly agrees. Has it paid off?

When Allstate observed its fiftieth anniversary in 1981, it reported $6.2 billion in revenues, $450 million in net income, $10.5 billion in assets, $2.8 billion in capital. Chairman Craib reports that Allstate earns over 15 percent on equity compared with the average for American industry of 10 to 11 percent, and has profit margins of 7 percent on sales compared with an all-industry average of approximately 4 percent. The "Good Hands" people seem to be just that.

The people at the top in these quality companies instinctively have a sensitive feeling for other people. If one were to examine their relationships with staff assistants, for example, they tend to have long-standing, loyal team partnerships with them. Many delegate a good deal of authority to their right hands because they believe deeply in a team effort. Team members working closely with CEOs naturally gain a keen sense of the shared chemistry and philosophy of the team.

In almost all cases there also is an inherent gentleness, a sense of common courtesy and respect for people, that shows through. When they interact with people at all levels it is evident that these leaders—who are also expert communicators—have a sense of wholeness about themselves. They are complete people. They have a strong sense of self, a desire to learn, to advance, to grow, to profit from their experiences.

They are not faultless. They make mistakes. They take risks. But they are true to certain ideals. Their sense of principle is high. They have a well-developed sense of outrage. Some have a low boiling point and can be quick to expose anger. Others have the skill, when the need presents itself, to criticize a subordinate without creating long-term resentment or deep personal injury.

Their language of communication is multifaceted. Some are excellent at expressing ideas orally. Some find it difficult to put their ideas on paper. Often this difficulty with writing stems from an educational or vocational background in engineering, finance, or production, where the timeworn strictures of the discipline have not cultivated the growth of polished communication skills. Good engineers are not necessarily good communicators. Financial officers often talk best through numbers. Plant managers are usually far better in personal interaction with people than in writing reports.

But all of these men and women have a special feeling for people that others readily sense. They have cultivated an attitude of caring about what is going on in the heads and hearts of people around them, and this makes them excellent team leaders. In large measure, their leadership ability springs from communication skills that are instinctive, gut-level, and have been learned under pressure either in the marketplace, in personal interaction, or in the not so gentle arena of negotiation. They have keenly cultivated instincts for sending messages and receiving vibrations from people that tend to be accurate.

We remember the instance when Oscar G. Mayer was the lone executive in Oscar Mayer & Co. who felt, solely based on his personal instinct for the marketplace, that a variety package of a half-dozen different cold cuts would be appealing to the consumer. Oscar Mayer & Co., even in the 1960s, had a sophisticated marketing research division replete with Ph.D.s and all the elaborate apparatus to test consumers' desires. The company spent a healthy $2.5 to $3 million per year on all forms of product research and development. All of the experts—the marketing vice president, the vice president for advertising and public relations, the general managers of plants, the product managers—said the variety-pack idea wouldn't sell.

Only Oscar G. Mayer, the chairman, believed it would, and the leader insisted that the product be produced and tried out in the marketplace. It was an instant success and still remains in the product line as testimony to good judgment and effective business leadership.

What is evident in this little vignette is the fact that communication, as we are using it in the context of corporate leadership, takes many forms. It need not be written or oral; it can be emotional, instinctive, and intellectual.

In some instances, a single symbol speaks more eloquently than words. We are thinking of the magnificent old oak tree that stands at the entrance to Deere & Company's handsome corporate headquarters in the rich prairieland of northwestern Illinois.

William A. Hewitt, when he was Deere's chairman, erected a plaque at the base of the tree in tribute to the architect, Eero Saarinen, masterful designer of the Deere corporate headquarters in Moline. The plaque reads:

> While selecting the site for these buildings Eero Saarinen was impressed by the trees he found here. This oak tree was his favorite. Today it is gratefully dedicated in his memory.

By this act of preservation, Deere's chairman sent a message to the thousands of farmers the company serves, to Deere's 60,000 employees and to all its friends and associates, that Deere is a special company that doesn't hide expressions of caring.

The New Campbell Soup

R. Gordon McGovern, the new president of Campbell Soup Co., hails from the marketing area. He was promoted out of Pepperidge Farm, considered by many business analysts the innovative side of stalwart Campbell Soup. Sixteen months into his tenure as president, a 30-year sales manager for Campbell echoes the nearly universal consensus in the company: "It's a brand new company. This guy is going to turn this company around."

His style: He sat unrecognized during his early days as president in the company cafeteria during the morning and afternoon coffee breaks and would prompt anyone from secretaries to chefs to tell him what was wrong with Campbell. And he listened. He hits the supermarkets and is not above finding out for himself by observing, straightening shelves of stock when a practiced eye notes cans out of line.

One time a store manager noted the fussing and straightening of shelves and inquired what was going on.

"That's the president of Campbell Soup," he was told by an accompanying sales executive traveling with McGovern.

Now, that's communication the customer understands.

The American Spirit

What of the American spirit and the national character in all of this? Is America in danger of being flim-flammed to death, and are the real values of our society being eroded away by the unending barrage of banality that sometimes masquerades as communication?

One of the nation's most distinguished journalists, Erwin D. Canham, when he was the editor of the *Christian Science Monitor,* met the issue head-on:

> Many books lately tell us we are being possessed by the organization. We are told that subtle advertising and public relations techniques, based upon depth psychology, are working their hidden persuasion well with us. Our public opinion is said to ebb and flow in massive waves. Our people are likened to the lemmings who rush over the cliff into the sea.
>
> I think this is largely nonsense. The minds of Americans have not been possessed. The reservoirs of common sense are still there. It is true, of course, that we are a big country in a period of mass communication. We need far greater diversity of ideas and diversity of communication. . . .
>
> The real rulers are still the people. The waves of ideas that sweep this nation may start from the most obscure corner, the most humble person, although they cover the nation by means of our mass communication network.
>
> Our task then, if we are to strengthen the fortresses of the mind, is to strengthen the moral sense. We can do that by exemplifying it.

We can strive for decency, honor, integrity in our own acceptance
and fulfillment of our life and professional responsibilities. Remember-
ing that our whole society depends upon the validity and the dignity
of individual men, we can live and act like men who believe in the
value of their lives and their society. We can inform a race of decision-
makers. We can help build an invincible society, even though today
we are tragically far from that goal. I believe we know what it is we
have to do.[25]

So spoke a masterful editor and communicator. His wise counsel
is still true today, and it will be true tomorrow.

PART TWO

Essence of the Crisis

CHAPTER 4

Work Alienation
and Love on the Job

The greatest task before civilization at present is to make
machines what they ought to be, the slaves, instead of the
masters of men.

Havelock Ellis

AMERICAN INDUSTRY has witnessed a parade of cookbook approaches to the problem of work alienation. Known by many labels—QWL (quality of work life), industrial democracy, quality circles, MBO (management by objectives), job enrichment, PDM (participative decision making)—over 30 of these programs have come and gone in the last 25 years. They have provided consultants and executives in the areas of human resource development, industrial relations, and public relations with a grab bag of managerial techniques. Many business and academic careers have been won and lost on such programs. Some of them have provided a temporary level of improvement in work attitudes. With very few exceptions, however, they haven't worked in U.S. factories and offices.

For managers who take the time to look, people experiencing work alienation in their businesses are abundant and easy to spot. Here is a glimpse of one of them.

In a large modern supermarket, part of a major chain in Minneapolis, we found the manager of the delicatessen department, Sidney Jacobson. He was quietly fussing over the cheese display, an expansive and impressive assortment that completely filled a commodious

51

refrigerated display case. His face appeared stern and his manner brusque. After several minutes of small talk, it became clear that Jacobson was upset about something. As our conversation progressed with questions and answers concerning the proper management of a deli department, he guardedly began to talk about what really was on his mind.

The problem seemed deceptively simple. After more than 20 years of experience in the delicatessen department, he believed, and rightly so, that he knew a great deal about how to display fine cheese properly. He felt strongly that a wedge of packaged cheese should be displayed simply and clearly, with no obstructing labels or price stickers obscuring the customer's view of the product. He believed that if necessary, a small label of black letters on gold foil could be used to identify the cheese on the upper left-hand corner of the package. He knew it was wrong, however, to place a gummy, poorly designed, and unattractive price label on the front surface of the cheese package. This was no trivial matter. It was Jacobson's job, his profession, his area of expertise.

As we continued to listen, we learned that the New York Stock Exchange–listed corporation that had recently acquired the locally owned store chain had decreed as central company policy that price stickers must go on the front of these packages. There would be no discussion and no exceptions would be allowed.

To Jacobson, this insistence on a foolish policy stood for everything he hated about the new corporation. Its professional managers had bought out the two-generation-family owners of his company and were now trying to tell him how to run his deli department. He was deeply angered. He didn't smile much at all anymore. Coworker relations had soured. The joy, the zest, and the fulfillment were gone from his work. What's more, his anger had begun to spill over into his family life, creating additional stress. Jacobson was struggling with the awful feeling of self-estrangement that accompanies work alienation. He felt no love in the workplace—and could give none.

In spite of its widespread existence, we know surprisingly little about work alienation. Almost nothing of any substance and genuine insight has been written and published about the subject since the late 1950s.[1]

And the problem is getting worse. While the causes of work alienation have never seemed clear, its symptoms—low productivity, dissatisfaction, withdrawal, poor product quality, high secrecy in the workplace—are clearly on the rise. Early forecasts suggest strongly that work alienation may reach an all-time high by the mid-1980s.

Why Bother?

American managers, especially those who are skeptical of the human resource development area in particular and the behavioral sciences in general, will often ask, "Why should I be concerned about employee attitudes? Does a positive job attitude increase productivity? Isn't this just a do-gooder humanitarian concern?" These are legitimate questions. They deserve straightforward answers.

The whole area of work attitudes has long held the attention of managers and management consultants. Over the past 50 years, there has been a flurry of interest in the subject of work satisfaction. During the same period, many organizations have developed programs with the purpose of measurably improving employee work attitudes. Sorting through all the available data is a time-consuming, difficult task. Yet it is essential that corporate leaders be well informed about current knowledge on the subject.

Alienation, like many other concepts in the organizational literature, lacks a consistent and specific definition. Academics and researchers can't quite agree on what alienation is. Research reports and articles in the professional journals frequently do not provide the reader with a clear definition of the concept. In some cases, differences in the findings among studies can be attributed to the fact that the researchers defined the concept differently and were probably, in fact, studying *different* factors. A wide variety of approaches to gathering and analyzing data on the subject of employee work attitudes has also contributed to the difficulty of adequately defining alienation. Collectively, the literature on employee attitudes presents the reader with a confusing array of arbitrarily chosen terms such as "worker morale," "job satisfaction," and "employee motivation."

The following discussion will seek to help clear the semantic fog surrounding the concept. Our objective is to address properly the "Why bother?" question.

In the work setting, an alienated person believes his or her behavior cannot determine the outcome he or she seeks. The word "believes" is an important part of this definition. One does not need to spend very much time in American factories and offices before coming to the conclusion that *work alienation is more than just job dissatisfaction.* It is not merely the frustration a person may feel as the result of an event on the job. It is a deep-seated emotional and intellectual conviction, the cumulative result of a series of negative work experiences. People do not choose to be alienated in the sense of choosing to be receptive or uncooperative. Alienation is a corrosive state of mind that eats away at people over a long period of time, often several years. It is both intense and pervasive.

Regardless of their place in the company hierarchy, alienated workers express one message clearly: They do not find fulfillment and meaning in their work. Their message is communicated in many different ways—absenteeism, pilferage, sabotage, a high degree of cynicism—but the message is always the same: "There is no fulfillment and meaning in my work." The seven items shown at the left of Figure 4.1, have been studied in numerous research programs over the past 50 years in the United States and western Europe.[2]

The straight-line, one-way arrows linking each factor with Fulfilling and Meaningful Work (F&MW) represent a causal relationship. The symbol appearing with each linkage (+, −, ?) indicates whether most studies have found this relationship to be positive (+), negative (−), or simply unclear (?).

Concerning the first causal factor—the work itself—most studies have found a positive relationship with F&MW. When employees view the work itself favorably, they also tend to view their job as being more satisfying.

Pay, the second variable, also appears to have a positive causal relationship with F&MW. This does not necessarily mean, however, that the greater the pay, the less one's alienation. Rather, it has been shown that when people perceive their pay as *equitable,* then this is one causal factor that tends to increase F&MW.

Skipping to the last three causal factors, the question marks indicate they do not appear to have a clear-cut relationship with F&MW. By themselves, these factors do not seem directly to increase or decrease it. Working conditions, for example, do not appear measurably to affect F&MW in most situations (the exception may be when working conditions are extremely poor or extremely good).

There has been a flurry of interest in demographics, the final factor. Demographic variables ordinarily studied include worker age, educational level, race, marital status, number of dependents, sex and urban/rural background. A motivating force behind this

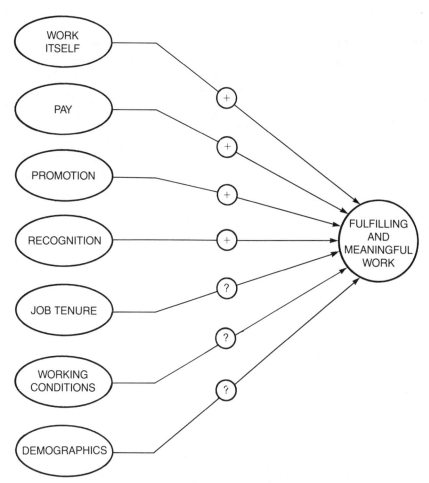

FIGURE 4.1   Causal Factors in Fulfilling and Meaningful Work: Events and Conditions

research has always been management's desire to identify and hire only those employees who, because of certain demographic characteristics, will tend to have better job attitudes. This research has not provided any clear-cut answers.

Figure 4.2 shows similar information for a second category of causal factors, agents.

Of particular interest is the fourth factor, management style. The question mark with the linkage indicates that research has not shown a consistently positive or negative relationship between management style and an F&MW experience on the part of employ-

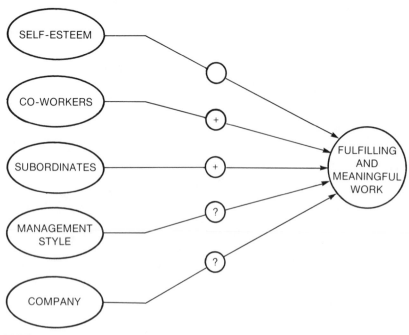

FIGURE 4.2   Causal Agents

ees. Contrary to popular opinion, a participative management style has not been shown to produce high job satisfaction in all situations; nor has an authoritarian style been shown consistently to result in job dissatisfaction. (Recent evidence suggests that the issue here is not management style at all, but rather management competence.) The management style factor was a particularly important variable in our study of worker attitudes in the automobile industry, mentioned in Chapter 2.

Let's address the "Why bother?" question more directly—what are the consequences of work alienation?

Figure 4.3 illustrates the relationship between Fulfilling and Meaningful Work and several end-result variables. The first two consequences, physical health and mental health, have been shown to be directly and positively influenced by F&MW. A growing number of studies are now examining coronary heart disease, level of serum cholesterol, and longevity, as well as overall mental health, as they relate to the concept of a positive job attitude.

The third consequence shown in Figure 4.3, productivity, is of special interest. Some researchers have proposed that the arrow goes the other way—that higher productivity actually produces

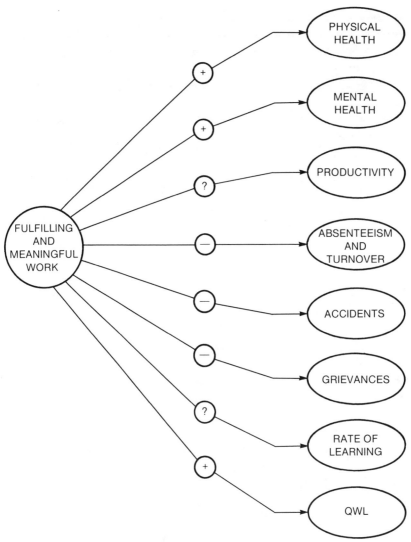

FIGURE 4.3   Consequences

changes in one's job attitudes. Whatever the nature of the relationship, it is probably affected by numerous other factors in the work environment, operating simultaneously. One salient point is clear: the research has not proven that happy workers are always more productive. Unhappiness can be a powerful motivator, too!

If a strong positive relationship between a good job attitude and productivity has not been proven conclusively, then *what tangible and practical justification is there for trying to improve work attitudes?* As indicated in Figure 4.3, absenteeism, turnover, and numbers of grievances as well as numbers of work-related accidents have been shown to be *lower* for employees with high F&MW. Also, the general quality of work life (QWL), or "climate" of the work environment, has been shown to *improve* with F&MW.

What Workers Want

For most American managers, even business and management educators, the use of the word "love" in connection with the workplace seems inappropriate. "Love" invariably brings to mind notions of romantic love or perhaps some un-businesslike religious teachings. These associations are so deeply ingrained into the consciousness and culture of traditional American management that it is extremely difficult for many persons to see beyond them. The thought of "loving relationships" makes most managers nervous and mildly embarrassed. But the love to which we refer in this chapter is neither romantic nor particularly religious. It is simply a form of relating to others effectively and in a genuinely caring manner.

American managers want to know, "What is it that employees want, anyway?" We believe the answer is clear, although it is not an easy answer; there is no stock, pat solution. Fulfilling and Meaningful Work experiences seem in every case to be characterized by four components: knowledge, care, respect, and responsibility. Erich Fromm used similar components to define the concept of love.[3] They form the acronym KCRR.[4]

Love on the Job

Knowledge is the answer to the question "What's going on?" For decades, enlightened managers have advocated that companies do more to help employees become more knowledgeable about all areas of the business, from production processes to market trends to awareness of the competition. The evidence is overwhelming: the time and effort it takes to help workers become knowledgeable about their work and about the business itself pays off for everyone concerned. We believe that one of the key differences between a good company and a great company is that a great company has a *knowledgeable* workforce.

Employees at all levels want to be able to address the question "What's going on?" Work alienation and lack of work knowledge seem to go hand in hand.

Some organizations create a bevy of communications devices— newsletters, magazines, letters from the president—without really *listening* to what it is that employees say they want to know. When asked about it, employees often say that they already have more information than they can handle. What's missing is a feeling of knowing how it all fits together, of understanding the meaning behind the facts and figures, of knowing "what's going on." Employees also want to know *why* management is taking certain actions. The "why factor" is thus a critical area of worker concern to address.

The fast-food industry provides a case in point. In large numbers, teenagers across America take their first jobs in fast-food restaurants. These jobs are plentiful, call for no prior work experience, and pay the minimum wage. These first work experiences, which contribute to the formation of a person's orientation toward work in general, are often negative. While a number of factors may account for the problem, clearly one of them is lack of work knowledge.

Fast-food employees often have absolutely no idea about what's going on beyond the rhythmic isolation of their own tasks. In some instances the restaurant manager, who is typically in his or her twenties, largely inexperienced and untrained, is the most alienated employee of all. Some of the fast-food chains are now designing and implementing new programs to help these people become more knowledgeable.

The point isn't that all employees must or even should know everything there is to know about the business, but basically that they need to *feel* they have sufficient knowledge to do their work as effectively as they possibly can. It is the employees themselves— not management—who must define the level of knowledge that will be sufficient, and this level will vary among people.

Care, the second component of KCRR, is the answer to the question "Who cares?" The desirable answer is "I do." Applied to work alienation, it means simply that "I care about what I do."

Sidney Jacobson, the supermarket delicatessen department manager described earlier, cared desperately about what he knew was the right way to display his cheeses. But his care did not register with the corporation that now owned his supermarket. Care is a two-way street. In Jacobson's case, it simply didn't care that he cared.

In Richard Ruch's study of the structure of employee attitudes in the automobile industry, 2,000 people were asked to respond to a series of questions about the nature of their work. "Caring about what I do" was named as a key reason for feeling good about coming to work each morning.[5] The frustration experienced by people who want to care about their work but don't, or can't because of long-standing unresolved conflicts, misunderstandings, misinformation, or lack of responsiveness to their caring attitude, is a key contributor to work alienation.

Respect, the third component, is the answer to the question "Why am I respected?"

In the work setting, one may feel respected for many reasons: job skills, superior performance, special credentials, a record of accomplishment, or status. In the context of work alienation, there is only one legitimate source of respect: one's *humanity.* This is why employees often tend to emphasize the "little things" when talking about the aspects of their work experiences that particularly affect their self-esteem. It has to do with such things as common courtesy among co-workers, feeling recognized as an individual, and being able to relate to other people in the workplace regardless of their particular role or status in the organization.

An executive acquaintance at General Motors Corporation illustrates this "need for respect because of humanity" principle in a little mock ritual we have seen him perform regularly as he comes into the office in the morning. Just before entering his office, he pauses before the office door. With great ceremony and flourish, he removes his hat and, placing it over his heart, faces Detroit for what he calls a "moment of meditation." By nature, this man is quiet and somewhat shy. His colleagues give a knowing smile as he performs his small ritual. To them it is a form of understatement with which they can identify. He seems to be saying, "I am a person, a unique individual, but I am also a good team player and I am going to inject a bit of humor into this thing."

Respect and care are probably the single most neglected aspects of American corporate leadership.

They are key concepts of successful work relationships, practiced with a studied ease by many Japanese managers, but regarded fearfully and timidly by the unenlightened. Using the concepts of respect and care effectively in work relationships, deliberately making them an active part of one's repertoire of communications skills, requires of the manager a certain amount of grace and flair, or what William

Ouchi has called *subtlety.*[6] *In essence, what we are talking about is showing respect for people's humanness by communicating that respect in subtle yet powerful ways.* This point warrants a minor digression.

Consider the all-important skill of active listening. This is generally not well understood by the typical manager, who may appreciate in a theoretical way the power of good listening but who has never received any training in this art and is not sensitized to the skillful finesse required to be a genuinely good listener.

Instead of passively absorbing words, the active listener concentrates on grasping the *facts* and *feelings* that are being communicated. To accomplish active listening, the listener must have the ability to communicate to the speaker that he or she understands the speaker's point of view. This requires not only listening to the words of a message but also listening to the feelings and attitudes being communicated and then responding to the speaker in such a way as to demonstrate that this additional information is being received. Sometimes, the feelings communicated are far more information-rich than the words used. To ignore the feelings would therefore result in missing the crux of the message.

The listener must be sensitive to communicated feelings in order to provide the kind of feedback to the speaker that constitutes active listening. *It cannot be faked.* Subtleties of expression contained in a single hesitation in speech, a change in voice tone and inflection, facial expressions and eye contact, and hand movements and breathing patterns may contain vast amounts of information.

Active listening requires intensive concentration. It is hard work. But it is a powerful way to communicate a sense of caring and respect from one person to another.

The fourth component of KCRR, *responsibility,* is the answer to the question "Am I accountable?" It doesn't particularly matter what one is accountable for (time, money, schedules) so long as one has a feeling of being *able* to be accountable.

This concept can be illustrated by the classic dilemma of "responsibility without commensurate authority." People caught in this trap are often alienated. It is difficult to have a feeling of responsibility in one's work without having at least some sense of control over its physical aspects—the resources and materials used, the work flow and pace of the work, the operations performed. Responsibility occurs when one has a holistic perspective of the work and a feeling of being accountable for one's own contribution.

Employees given the freedom to decorate their work area to their own taste feel good about that thoughtful degree of flexibility. An opportunity to express one's own individuality by hanging a favorite picture, bringing in a plant, or displaying other personal effects contributes in a small but meaningful way to that sense of having control over one's destiny that is so important to employees.

Little wonder that worker alienation thrives in the sterile environment of identical work areas devoid of any sign of humanity other than homage to the dull repetition of the master planner's ultimate tribute to boredom and monotony.

These four components—knowledge, care, respect, and responsibility—are absolutely necessary for a work experience that is fulfilling and meaningful, regardless of the particular nature of the work itself or the particular status of the job or its location in the organizational hierarchy. Alienation, as we have defined it, is a state of self-estrangement. The components of alienation are person-bound, not situation-bound. There is no place to hide in relation to KCRR; no organizational development gimmicks are needed to bring it about, just serious individual and personal commitment to the principles of KCRR.

Seek and You Shall Find

A set of mutual expectations, varying in degree of explicitness, seems to affect every employee/employer relationship.[7] A typical organization, for example, expects that its employees come to work on time, be willing to work overtime occasionally, be dressed appropriately for the job, not abuse coffee breaks, and fulfill a host of other worksetting expectations. More severely, some employers might expect that employees join certain community groups, give a fixed amount to particular company-endorsed charities, and not purchase the products of competitors.

An individual employee, on the other hand, might expect to be treated as an adult, receive recognition for superior work, enjoy reasonable job security, and be able to use all his or her skills and abilities on the job. More extremely, some employees might expect that the employer provide means for personal growth and development, allow vacations to be scheduled at the employee's convenience, and tolerate certain personal habits and idiosyncracies that may affect the work.

The degree to which these mutual expectations are specifically communicated is crucial to determining whether or not there is KCRR in the workplace. If these expectations remain unarticulated, they will be communicated in other forms, such as absenteeism, turnover, and other manifestations of work alienation.

Unfortunately for both the employee and the employer, explicit communication of expectations often does not occur during the hiring process and thereafter. Specific expectations remain unarticulated for several different reasons: lack of communications skills, fear of conflict, unawareness of the importance of communication, lack of motivation to communicate expectations, or a company style of secretiveness.

Whatever the reasons, the lack of explicit communication about the expectations often stands directly in the way of finding KCRR on the job.

The tone for open and explicit communication in any organization is set by the people at the top. By their example and reputations, real and imagined, by their perceived track records, the climate for communication and the unwritten rules for patterns of interaction are set forth for the whole organization. *In too many companies, top executives wrongly assume that subordinates have an accurate view of the personal style they wish to project as communicators.* What they want to project and what is actually perceived by others are frequently not the same thing. The dual images are not focused, the facts not congruent.

What the CEO wants to project as a communication style is typically an ideal that is not actually lived up to in day-to-day business interaction. It's the projection of this *ideal* communication style that is so vital.

Nobody expects a chief executive always to practice what he or she preaches. But what is preached, if it is real and sincere, will go a long way in setting the tone for communication that subordinates will feel they should follow. Effective communication can't be faked, but too many CEOs fail to make clear the kind of communicator they would like to be. When this ideal is regularly and sincerely set forth so others can see it and feel it, then a high standard is established and everyone has something worthwhile to strive for. For the CEO who doesn't make it a regular part of his or her job to talk about good communication, about the high ideals of openness and honesty in human interaction, an essential part of effective leadership sadly will be neglected *and no one will know that somebody at the top actually cared about it.*

We have argued here that work alienation is keyed to a lack of KCRR. In large part, this is a communication problem. Its solution does not call for the fancy trappings of expensive and glossy employee newsletters or an elaborate video information network with computer terminals in every office. The plain truth about KCRR is that it is not so much something to be *given* to employees as it is something they need to *find* in their work experiences.

Perhaps the greatest challenge to corporate leadership in America today is to establish conscious programs to enable the millions of alienated workers, in factories and offices across the country, to realize KCRR in and from their work.

CHAPTER 5

Management Education and the MBA Myth

*If a little knowledge is dangerous, where is the man who
has so much as to be out of danger?*

Thomas Henry Huxley

THE VAST MAJORITY of managers in American corporations lack
a comprehensive and enlightened view of communication—a view
that could translate into more effective leadership and ultimately
a more effective and profitable organization. Almost all managers
are vaguely aware of the importance of good communication and
are quick to pay lip service to "communication problems" in their
companies. For the most part, this appreciation of the importance
of good communication is superficial. The executive who understands the power available to him or her in the form of communication is a rarity.

By any assessment, business school education and executive corporate training are not providing sufficient preparation in communication skills. Nor are they providing substantive educational experiences that give the student or executive the opportunity to develop
an enlightened understanding of the communication process as it
applies to the modern corporation. This lack of preparation runs
deep into the classic traditions of business and management education, including not only the business school curriculum, which is
lacking in courses in communication, but also the skills and knowl-

edge of the faculty, who typically do not have much of a background in corporate communication.

The problem goes beyond MBA (master of business administration) degree programs. It also encompasses all of business and management education, including the vast network of corporate executive training programs in the United States. But there is no question that the MBA degree is the standard credential for those who aspire to upper management positions in American business. Thus we will focus our attention here.

The MBA Boom

MBA students—some 250,000 of them in approximately 1,200 master of business administration programs across the country—are, according to a recent newsmagazine headline, the "new elite on campus." More than 60,000 of them are to receive their degrees in 1983, compared with about 5,000 in 1960. MBA enrollments have now surpassed the traditionally large professional programs in fields such as law and engineering.

Contrary to common opinion, the popularity of the MBA is not a recent development. The large enrollment increases in MBA programs across the country are not merely a flash in the pan, reflecting the changing whims of student interest. Growth in business enrollments, especially at the MBA level, has been sustained for 25 years.

The MBA boom has been a mixed blessing for American business. The good news is that MBAs are very well prepared in the technical areas of business administration—in accounting, management information systems, finance, and operations management. *As a group, MBAs are intelligent, motivated to enter into the corporate mainstream, eager to accept responsibility.* The bad news is that while the typical MBA may be a master of technique, he or she is often lacking when it comes to substance, especially in the nontechnical areas.[1]

Lewis H. Young, editor-in-chief of *Business Week,* has brought the problem into clear focus:

> Business has fallen prey to the same stultifying force of bureaucratization that makes government ponderous, unresponsive and paralyzed. Some people blame the malaise on the education drummed into students at graduate school of business. In training the MBA to be number

oriented, the curriculum puts minimum value on intuition and the feel of the business. In teaching MBAs to minimize risk, the courses discourage them from attempting the new project that can bring big rewards. In teaching MBAs how to analyze problems thoroughly, the schools ignore the need to implement solutions to those problems. And in importing such sophisticated tools of management as strategic planning, portfolio management and computer services, the colleges ignore the basics of management which have to do with motivating people.[2]

Higher education in general is going through rough times. As we enter the mid-1980s, the available pool of traditional college students is diminishing. Government cuts in support of higher education have hurt both state-supported and private institutions. Salaries for college and university professors have been seriously eroded by inflation, even more so than for secondary and elementary public school teachers. It is no secret that many insiders believe the quality of the educational experience provided by our nation's colleges and universities has been declining. John Slaughter, director of the National Science Foundation, recently stated "there is no question that the U.S. in its educational system has fallen behind many of the countries we need to be competing with."[3]

In business schools, the continuing proliferation of "off-campus" MBA programs with low admission requirements, few Ph.D.s on the faculty, no libraries, no computer facilities, and recruitment-driven curricula constitute a prime example of the unfortunate trend in many quarters of higher education to maximize tuition revenue at the expense of program quality. Even at many well-established universities, it has become difficult for some business school deans to maintain program quality. Where overall university enrollments are in a state of decline, the business school is often pressured to "open up" the MBA program. Consequently, admission standards may be eased, average class sizes may swell to 100 students per section, and the energy of the faculty may become disproportionately concentrated on processing students. Questions of curriculum improvement, program quality, and innovation become secondary in such an environment.

Clearly, there is still much to admire about business school education and its flagship degree program, the MBA. The business curriculum is generally rigorous, demanding performance from students in a number of different disciplines—mathematics, statistics, behavioral science, economics, and law. Doctoral programs in the business administration fields are also stringent, requiring serious commitment and dedication from those who aspire to a career as a business professor. Faculty salaries in business schools, although hard hit by inflation, are 20 to 50 percent higher than those in other departments around the campus, especially in the arts and humanities, and there is currently a severe shortage of doctorally qualified business professors. The steady demand for business graduates has continued strong for several decades, and students with good academic records still receive multiple job offers.

Good business schools have long sought to set up a reasonable balance between the professional and technical courses in business and courses in the liberal arts and sciences. This balance has traditionally been a big point in selling the value of a business school education, not without some justification. Likewise, good business faculty are sensitive to the need to reach the "whole person." Business schools that have achieved accreditation by the American Assembly of Collegiate Schools of Business (AACSB) require of all their students that between 40 and 60 percent of their coursework be taken outside of the business school. This so-called 40/60 rule of the AACSB is specifically intended to help ensure that business students get a healthy dose of introductory courses in the social sciences, literature, and the natural sciences in addition to their business courses. But here's the catch: the AACSB's minimum standards for accreditation are very stringent, difficult to meet, and largely inflexible. Consequently, the vast majority of American business schools are not accredited by AACSB. In fact, of the approximately 1,200 MBA programs in the United States, less than 20 percent are AACSB-accredited.

Hard Drives Out Soft

Most business schools make an attempt to provide at least some treatment of the area of business ethics in a course called Business and Society, a relatively new discipline within the standard business school curriculum that concerns itself with the interface between business organizations and the larger society. In recent years, business faculty have given increased attention (albeit slowly) to this kind of course in the MBA program. The American business track record, after all, is not pristine when it comes to unethical and illegal corporate practice. In the last decade, 117 major U.S. corporations were caught breaking the laws,[4] irregular business activities are regularly reported in the news media, and it is no news that questionable industrial espionage activities are often condoned by business executives. Ostensibly, Business and Society is a course that attempts to address the dilemma of "how to ensure a functionally high level of obedience to organizational authority while preventing excessively high levels of obedience that are dysfunctional for society."[5]

The Business and Society course is exemplary of some of the right-thinking characteristics of the better MBA programs in the United States. For the most part, however, the impact of this course has been diminished because it is usually taught by a member of the business school faculty who holds a Ph.D. degree in a business discipline but lacks depth in the areas of sociology, philosophy, and history.

Peter Drucker is one of a relatively small number of educators who have been instrumental in trying to broaden the thinking behind business school education. Drucker, considered by thousands of managers to be a professor of management, is actually Clarke Professor of Social Sciences at Claremont Graduate School. He has written persuasively about the demand in professional education for "a humanistic perspective that can integrate advanced professional and technical knowledge into a broader universe of experience and learning."[6] James Hayes, chairman of the board of American Management Associations, likes to make the same plea this way: Of the 168 clock hours in a week, assume we use about 40 hours for work and another 70 hours for sleeping and eating. That leaves 58 hours. In business schools, says Hayes, we ought to be more concerned about the quality of those 58 hours.[7]

Writing in the *New York Times* business section recently, a second-year MBA student criticized the typical business curriculum for not sufficiently emphasizing the social purpose and responsibilities of capitalism, and chided business school faculty members for teaching how to make money but not how to be humane. He seriously questioned the "me first" attitude he saw developing in his fellow students, and asked what would happen when they entered the business world lacking an enlightened appreciation of the relationship between our economic and social systems. The question rings in our ears. It is the same question asked from the pages of Peter Cohen's little volume *The Gospel According to the Harvard Business School,* a chilling story about how the premier B-school's "blind faith in competition alienates its students from one another, driving them to the destructive selfishness, the 'rugged individualism' that, for too long, has been mistaken for the mainspring for progress."[8]

Too many business school administrators, faculty members, and executives from the business community that supports the business school fall into the trap of believing that study in the arts, sciences, and humanities has little functional place in the business curriculum beyond a token smattering of low-level introductory courses. One of the outstanding scholars who has eloquently addressed this issue is S. I. Hayakawa, who argued in his classic *Language in Thought and Action:*

> The study of history and literature, therefore, is not merely the idle acquisition of social polish, as practical men are fond of believing, but a necessary means of both increasing our communications with others and of increasing our understanding of what others are trying to communicate to us.[9]

The principle at work here is captured in the simple phrase "Hard drives out soft," coined by Harvard Business School professor Louis Barnes, a sensitive and insightful business educator. Barnes is a veteran of the battlefield of Harvard Business School faculty meetings, where he has eloquently represented the unpopular view that business students should be grappling with such "soft" subjects as trust. The irony of "Hard drives out soft" is that the so-called hard subjects of business school education—finance, accounting, operations management—are the easy ones to teach and to learn. The so-called soft subjects—communication, business ethics, social responsibility—are the toughest ones to teach and to learn. They require more teaching skill than most business schools can cultivate or are willing to develop in this time of economic and intellectual depression in higher education. When push comes to shove, soft subjects are usually interdisciplinary, requiring cooperation among colleagues representing different disciplines from within and outside the business school. Such cooperative efforts require visionary leadership, the kind provided by individuals who thrive on intellectual adventure and experimentation. Such individuals are no longer plentiful in our business schools (which are often branded as elitist and uncooperative on their own campuses) for many have left academe for greener pastures.

MBAs from Harvard alone head more than 3,500 U.S. corporations, far more than from any other business school, and they represent 19 percent of the top three officers in the Fortune 500.[10] Both of us have spent time there, lived on the campus, and counseled Harvard MBAs who are CEOs, and one of us has been taught by some of the master teachers on the Harvard Business School's staff, including Louis Barnes. The MBA myth, which is nothing more than the unfailing belief that the MBA *as it stands* is the perfect preparation for a career in business and management, is not specific to any one institution. The myth pervades the whole business culture worldwide.

Why J. P. Can't Write

Employers and recruiters have for years been demanding of business schools, "Give us students who can communicate." College and university business programs have been slow to respond and often have responded with no more than a token revision of the standard freshman composition course. The demand for better teaching and more meaningful courses in the area of communication is well documented. *Fortune* magazine recently reported that employers surveyed said they wanted business schools to do a better job teaching their students communication skills. Similarly, a recent Conference Board study of 610 major U.S. corporations showed that lack of adequate communication skills was the most common problem cited by personnel executives in their dealings with new employees. The Association of MBA Executives in its newsletter, *MBA Executive,* explains that "those MBAs whose communication skills are superior have had and will continue to have a considerable advantage in their careers, regardless of the industry in which they choose to work." When asked, graduates of MBA programs themselves who have been out in the world of work for a few years consistently name one area that they think should receive more emphasis in formal business education—communication.[11]

This shortcoming in management education has been evident for a long time. A small number of business educators, such as William V. Muse, now vice chancellor for academic affairs at Texas A&M and the former business school dean there, have tried to make the problem more visible to the business community. Reflecting on his many years as a business school dean, Muse has written about the "continuing lack of willingness or ability on our part to focus our energies on developing the skill most lacking, yet most desired, by our graduates—the ability to communicate. After at least 20 years of complaining by industry recruiters," Muse observes, "we don't seem to have progressed much at all, or even given communication skills a high priority."[12]

America's business schools continue to turn out graduates who are inept communicators. Evidence of this is overwhelming and widely acknowledged, even by business school graduates themselves. When a stab is occasionally taken at teaching communication skills in a business school, it frequently winds up reinforcing the double-talk and jargon. The value of open, honest, and straightforward communication to the function of the executive turns out to be a very difficult lesson to teach and to learn. Most business school professors readily admit that they are not equipped with the training and do not possess the skills necessary to teach effective communication to their students. And because "hard drives out soft," they are not particularly motivated to try.

English departments have been attempting to teach communication skills to business, technical, and professional students for many years. Essentially, what they have done is taken the standard English composition course and injected into it writing assignments based on hypothetical business situations, assuming this scheme would grab the business student's attention and provide a basic foundation in "practical English." Whether they're called Business Writing, Technical Writing, or Industrial Reporting, the evidence is that students who take these courses show no significant improvement in writing ability over control groups who don't take the courses. Stated another way, the truth is that college writing courses don't work.[13] Some studies have even shown that required public speaking courses regularly fail to achieve skill improvement for students who exhibit high communication apprehension, or "stage fright." Such findings seem to fly in the face of the assumption that a course in oral communication is worthwhile if for no other reason than to help business students learn how to cope with stage fright when they stand up before a group of peers.[14] The task of teaching communication skills should never have been given to English departments in the first place. The pecking order in English departments long ago relegated the teaching of composition to the bottom rung of the professorial ladder of status. The best English professors are usually not the ones who specialize in English composition.

Teaching composition is awful work. What's worse, many composition teachers are closet authors who haven't yet made it into print. In this regard, they are very much like the junior high school band directors who cringe on every sour note, fantasizing about what it would be like if there were real musicians in the room with them.

The regrettable truth in the face of all of this is that the typical business school curriculum tolerates only one or two courses in communication skills. Of all those twelve hundred or so MBA programs across the nation, only a very few of them have even one course in communication skills as part of the required curriculum. In fact, a recent study of what 17 leading graduate business programs offer in this subject area showed that only four schools—Dartmouth, Harvard, Tulane, and Virginia—require all students to take a separate course for credit in writing and speaking skills. And only four others require such a course for students who do not pass a proficiency exam on writing and/or speaking skills.[15] Obviously, this is not sufficient.

What is to be done? What is the pathway out of the quagmire of the inarticulate business manager?

Right now the call must go out for educational revival in business schools. The standard business school curriculum is too technical, too traditional, and lacks innovation and experimentation. It is simply not fertile breeding ground for the development and nurturing of leadership ability. Business education yearns for a new dawning; the old curriculum has been much too slow to change, and then has only changed in format, not in substance. Present-day business school education may have been appropriate 25 years ago, but not today. The backlash of the turbulent 1960s in higher education, when experimentation was the name of the game and everything was questioned for its "relevance," has brought us to a virtual standstill in program enrichment. We need to break the cult of the quantitative elitist in business schools—who have oversold American business on the value of numbers-oriented decision making—through a unique working partnership among enlightened educators, visionary business leaders, and scientists, artists, and humanists outside of education. Carl Sagan, in his *Dragons of Eden,* has written about the remarkably gifted multidisciplinary scientists and scholars who are sometimes referred to as polymaths, and the marvelous contributions they have made to human knowledge and understanding. Britain has produced a number of these individuals, such as Bertrand Russell, Alfred North Whitehead, and Jacob Bronowski. "Particularly today," writes Sagan, "when so many difficult and complex problems face the human species, the development of broad and powerful thinking is desperately needed." Instead, he laments, we find in formal education "an almost reptilian ritualization of the educational process."[16] In short, we need to combine resources and initiate a true revival in business education, with the goal of nurturing the development of the polymath.

The Council for the Advancement of Experimental Learning (CAEL) broke new ground in 1981 in publishing a slim volume entitled *Business and Higher Education: Toward New Alliances.*[17] The book is an important first attempt to provide a framework for bringing together more effectively the efforts and resources of both industry and institutions of higher education in the name of training and education. Both sides are deeply into the same game when it comes to business and management education, and it is high time they collaborated more successfully. Corporate training is actually a second system of education in the United States, representing a huge financial investment, estimated at $50 billion annually. The Bell System alone spent $1.7 billion on employee education in 1980. The total spent by our 3,500 colleges and universities is estimated at $55 billion annually. The CAEL has challenged America to consider the powerful impact of combining at least some of these resources in ways that are mutually beneficial.

The impetus for these changes will probably not originate from within our nation's business schools. American corporations could initiate the call for this business educational revival, for they are the benefactors and beneficiaries of business education. They hold more than just financial clout, loudly as that may speak to business school deans. The thinking, ideas, and knowledge that come from experience are vital resources to business education. The presence of a corporate executive on campus commands the attention of faculty and administrators. Those 250,000 MBA students are engaged in basic training for management careers. The extent to which they will be successful after graduation, as executives and as adults, will be greatly determined by the quality of the educational experiences provided by American business schools. Successful business managers hold tremendous power—much more than they typically realize—to influence the course of education for American corporate leadership.

It is time to begin to use that power.

CHAPTER 6

The Classic Charade
in Corporate Communication

*I come from a State that raises corn and cotton and cockle-
burs and Democrats, and frothy eloquence neither convinces
nor satisfies me. I am from Missouri. You have got to show
me.*

Willard Duncan Vandiver

C HESTER BARNARD, in his 1938 classic book on business management, *The Functions of the Executive,* made the powerful point
that communication lies at the heart of managerial success.[1] Yet
today more than ever in the history of corporate life, good communication is becoming increasingly rare in business and industry. How
can this be?

Let's look at some of the facts. In a cover story on "The Company
Image" in *Business Week* a few years ago, a survey was reported
showing that 60 percent of America's CEOs do not trust their own
communications officers.[2]

Irving Kristol, writing in the *Wall Street Journal* on "Ethics
and the Corporation," explains why:

> The point is that American corporations do have a critical problem
> with public opinion, and to cope with this problem spend tens of
> millions of dollars a year on "public relations." Yet a number of these
> corporations then proceed to behave in such a way as to offend and
> outrage the corporation's natural constituency: the stockholders. More
> important, the business community as a whole remains strangely pas-
> sive and silent before this spectacle. This disquieting silence speaks

far more eloquently to the American people than the most elaborate public relations campaign. And it conveys precisely the wrong message.

Indeed, one of the reasons the major corporations find it so difficult to persuade the public of anything is that the public always suspects them of engaging in clever public relations, instead of simply telling the truth. And the reason the public is so suspicious is because our large corporations so habitually do engage in clever public relations instead of simply telling the truth.[3]

Business leaders have to bear the responsibility for correcting these wrongs and keeping faith with the 30 million American shareholders who own the nation's industry and business. They must accept responsibility for the erosion of trust this charade is producing, which threatens the vitality of American corporate life.

Corporate officers, who are paid to be effective business leaders and consequently should be good business communicators, have failed in handling well their responsibility of transmitting ideas to their various constituencies. They have become almost immune to the plaintive outrages of employees and consumers. Within their own companies they have become so enmeshed in protective barriers that screen them from contact with the workforce that they are all but cut off from the reality of what their employees are saying, thinking, and feeling.

All this at a time when the expenditure for corporate communication in America is constantly rising and by 1985 may reach $40 billion.

The Worst Communicators

If one were to compile a hit list of the worst communicators in industry, the accounting would surely contain the big oil companies, the public utility companies, banks, insurance companies, and financial service organizations. To this list must be added the health care industry.

Poor communication in the health care industry is epidemic. Can you recall a truly good job being done in a busy general hospital of informing the community it serves about the reasons for the wildly escalating increases in the costs of a hospital room and other in-hospital services? America's health care business in 1981 was a

$287 billion industry and for the past 15 years has had an annual growth rate of 13 percent (15.1 percent in 1981 alone). Health care expenditures represent 9.8 percent of the GNP. Yet hospitals are inept at reporting honestly and openly to their constituencies.

In a survey we conducted a few years ago we found newspaper editors, beat reporters covering hospitals, and the newsmen on radio and television were all frustrated by the cloak of secrecy many hospitals maintain.[4] One bitter managing editor called it "a closed society dominated by the doctors who run the hospital for their private gain." Others, particularly in the television news-gathering side of the business, lamented that whenever there was a disaster or a serious accident of major proportions, no hospital administrator was ever around who could clear vital facts. Reporters said they inevitably get the runaround when they try to gather news of a prominent citizen being treated in a hospital. Of course, we understand the rights of the patient to privacy and the obligations of the physician and the hospital to protect patient rights, but does it have to degenerate to license to say nothing?

Our study showed extreme willingness of hospitals to talk to the press when money is to be raised for a new wing, or to buy a new, more expensive cardiac unit, often when the hospital across the street has the same duplicated facilities.

"But just try and get permission to sit in on a trustees meeting when they are debating a steep raising of prices," a hospital beat reporter comments. "No one wants to talk, and there is an invisible conspiracy to secrecy. When we dig and piece together our story, then they howl if we have an inadvertent error in a number because no one was willing to be quoted."

We have been schooled on the belief that the man at the top is there to "give the lady what she wants," in the words of Chicago's Marshall Field & Company. Though this may once have been true, in today's world of computerized business in which a machine generates form letters untouched by human hands, it is nearly impossible for the customer to talk to the people at the top.

Yet an unending parade of expensive corporate advertising urges us to read company annual reports and to send in for their position papers on burdensome taxes. We are asked to speak up and help Company X fight too restrictive safety legislation imposed by senseless Washington bureaucrats. But just try to be heard when telling your story about how its product or service has gone awry.

Good Management Cultivates Good Communication

The best companies treat people decently—both their customers and their employees—and they have a real magic in not fouling up along the way."[5] So says Thomas J. Peters, a business organization specialist at the Stanford University Business School.

He has studied the characteristics of companies that generally are setting the standards of quality in their fields. He found that the magic of all of the great companies is that they do not ignore the customer or quality. They never give in to bureaucracy. They cater to people's natural desire to be associated with good products, not junk. His list of top companies now numbers 75 and includes such famous names as Hewlett-Packard, Texas Instruments, Emerson Electric, Fluor, Procter & Gamble, Boeing, and IBM.

These excellent companies are found to have common characteristics basic to good communication:

- A commitment to doing instead of just talking.
- Close customer contact at all levels of management.
- Autonomy to encourage the spirit of entrepreneurship.
- Orientation toward people rather than numbers.
- Stress on value of quality even if it means being second in product development rather than risk a less superior product.
- Rigid quality controls in all operations.
- Lean staffs.

Fundamental to any good communication effort in almost any setting is a commitment to openness and honesty. The CEO who makes this commitment is willing to absorb the costs of communicating genuinely with *all* constituencies—large and small, powerful or weak. This is the first real move toward creating a great company. Such CEOs take their leadership responsibilities seriously—and they communicate well. The business results show it, both at the bottom line and in the respect and admiration these CEOs are accorded from employees, customers, and their peers.

Listen to the philosophy of an athlete turned business executive.

James Daniell, who was captain of the Cleveland Browns football team in 1945, runs a company in Niles, Ohio—RMI Co. Since taking control of RMI, Daniell has boosted sales 500 percent from 1976 levels. In late 1978 the company reported its first quarterly profit in four years. At the heart of this dramatic turnaround was a Daniell philosophy of good communication and healthy proliferation of smiles and personal warmth and genuine caring for the employees.

Daniell says, "Believe it or not, for a big, dumb football player, I have a philosophy. 'Do unto others as you would have them do unto you.' "[6]

Charles Corman, president of the Clerical and Technical Union local, says of CEO Daniell's style and philosophy, "He calls us into meetings and lets us know what's going on, which is unheard of in other industries."

Robert Paul, a Lockheed Corporation vice president and RMI customer, calls the Daniell method a "management approach this whole country needs to get production up."

Disenchantment at the Top

There is no question that many chief executives today are disenchanted with their companies' communication efforts. Yet most major companies have whole departments or even divisions committed to communications tasks. Why are these departments failing so miserably? One answer is evident in what is happening inside the professional society of communications practitioners.

The Public Relations Society of America, Inc., headquartered in New York City, has 12,000 members. It is 35 years old and feels it is the premier professional group in the United States. A few years ago it gave birth to a Professional Development program. PRSA is having to work hard to get its members to take the Professional Development program seriously. It's putting renewed vigor into a national membership drive in the face of escalating costs and is watching with wonderment as its student society—PRSSA, now with 120 chapters—grows by hundreds of student members each year.

The bright, questioning, and alert students wanting to come into the professional practice of public relations are in many cases more inquiring and willing to work harder than their elders. We find these young would-be practitioners to be the cream of a new crop of future professionals. They are sorely needed in corporate

America. When we see them clamoring for practical information and absorbing ideas at the annual conference of PRSA and at various regional seminars and meetings, we are proud of their vigor and interest.

Would that one could be as proud of the rank and file of the nation's public relations directors, not only in business and industry but in the not-for-profit sector and in government too. By and large, over the course of many years of observing the nature of corporate practitioners in communications, we have found these people, while conscientious and hard-working, to be one-dimensional. They tend to see their responsibility largely in terms of press clippings and what the media are doing to them or saying about them. Their ability to be corporate strategists is minimal. While there are some communications officers who are sound strategists, have earned their way to the senior management conference table, and are listened to with respect, too many of the public relations directors we know or have seen in operation tend to be relegated to second-class citizenship in today's corporate leadership structure.

Why? In many instances they are ill prepared for their growing responsibilities. Most still tend to be oriented toward print communication. By far the greatest proportion of professional public relations practitioners are trained in journalism. Their ranks are filled with men and women who were weaned on newspaper work, or were magazine writers or editors or broadcasters. However good these backgrounds may be in expressing one's ideas on paper or in well articulating thoughts in oral form, the profession still suffers from too little emphasis on business training and scholarship. Competent communicators with degrees in economics, finance, or political science, with skills and knowledge in sociology, psychology, and professional counseling or human services, would seem to have more appropriate backgrounds for a career so inherently people-oriented.

We have long felt that a divinity degree would be an ideal background for a counselor to a CEO in corporate communication. A theologian would be an invaluable ally in dealing with matters of corporate ethics and business morality. Merely scanning the daily press reveals frequent episodes of corporate life fraught with challenges that call for a discipline akin to that of a broad-gauged religious thinker or a philosopher whose beliefs are rooted in pragmatism. The problems business leaders have to deal with and communicate about to large audiences are of such scope and complexity that the analytical skills and the scholarship of a historian are often called for. Indeed, an Arthur Schlesinger, the Pulitzer-prize-winning historian, would make a splendid communicator in the modern corporate world. Mastering the essay form and being schooled in the great literature of our heritage are excellent preparation for careers in the new communication excellence we urge business to insist upon. Studying the great masters' prose, poetry, and drama would enrich and raise the creative output of business.

Our colleagues who are in corporate communication posts today can be faulted for often being:

- one-dimensional—thinking only in print terms;

- not research-oriented;

- short on advanced educational training or thin on professional development;

- not interested in practicing a more holistic approach to communication in business;

- given to overstatement rather than the practice of a more conservative approach;

- too quick to assume that good communication is a panacea that can be used as a substitute for sound management;

- simplistic at times in ignoring some of the overall dimensions of the total corporation in favor of narrow tunnel vision;

- prone to believe their own hyperbole to the point where at times they lose sight of the horizon.

These comments are not made to harass the craft and its able practitioners, but to face up to the reality of the problems that have been created in the field of communication over the past two decades. Other disciplines are being called upon by the CEO, in desperation, for help in crucial communication decision making and strategy formulation. It is because of the inadequacies of the professional communicators that lawyers, accountants, engineers, scientists, and marketing professionals are being dragooned into service as the CEO's alter ego for communication. It is high time to regroup, retrain, and restructure.

Nuclear Communication Folly

Consider the following example of the serious consequences that result when a company loses control of the communication process: On March 29, 1979, the Three Mile Island nuclear mishap occurred. The next day, the Arizona Atomic Energy Commission sent a notice to one of our clients—American Atomics Corporation, in Tucson—that it was in violation of fourteen of the Commission's rules for handling tritium gas. Tritium is a low-level, beta-particle-emitting by-product of the federal government's nuclear energy program. It is used in private manufacturing to energize tiny glass tubes coated internally with phosphor. The beta particles excite the phosphor to luminescence and the sealed tubes give off an eerie but useful green or yellow light. They have a "half life" of 12.3 years, which means they burn constantly for a dozen years and produce low-level safe illumination without batteries, wires, or bulbs—an ideal product for a country in an energy crunch. Our client manufactured "Chronolites," tiny laser-sealed Pyrex tubes, which were used to illuminate the face of digital wrist watches and to make exit signs for public buildings. This practical line of products evolved from years of research by a group of scientists who enlisted private investors to fund the R & D program.

Arizona authorities alleged that harmful emissions of tritium gas were released into the air in the residential neighborhood where the small company was located. A public hearing was called and the media jumped on the story, especially because a school lunchroom nearby was found to have "contaminated" food. CBS News then picked up the story nationally, and that triggered a media circus. Despite evidence produced by the company's management that no harmful violations of public safety or employee safety were involved, the plant's license to handle the materials was suspended.

Arizona Governor Bruce Babbitt ordered the Arizona National Guard into the American Atomics plant to seize the gas, subsequently found to be harmless and stored safely in steel containers, and trucked it off to a military dump where it was buried.

The little $8 million company was forced to file for bankruptcy, and 200 workers were thrown out of jobs.

Here is what the *Tucson Citizen* said editorially:

> The press and the electronic media played an important and regrettable role in fanning popular apprehensions.
>
> The result of emotion, publicity, politics and lack of consensus

is that a firm that tried to play by the rules has been forced to close. Many Tusconians have had to find other jobs.

The American Atomics saga does nobody credit.[7]

Add to this the words of *New York Times* science writer Malcolm Brown that the nuclear accident at Three Mile Island was "one of the worst disasters in American journalistic history. We saw there the kind of mob scene that makes it impossible to get at the truth. It was like a lynch mob."[8]

Such an episode could be repeated tomorrow in communities across the country. Yet, to our knowledge, no one has committed any funds or research effort to solve this type of "nuclear disaster" communication problem even though we live in a Nuclear Age.

In many respects, the professionals in the public relations field seem to feel comfortable being behind the times. When the chips are down and a plant closing is contemplated, for instance, it is the operating managers who call the shots. Plant general managers end up dictating policy on news dissemination, and thus often the wrong emphasis is used in planning distribution of news to the workers and other parties involved. In too many such cases, a plant is closed and the employees first hear about it in the local newspaper or on the TV evening news.

As events over the years have shown time and again, when hard decisions must be made affecting manufacturing operations or facilities in local communities, the communication pros are either not consulted or their advice is not heeded. Such lessons as the wisdom of dealing gently, sympathetically, and sensitively with plant closings and layoffs are often learned the hard way.

Where are the humanistically oriented communicators when such notices are distributed first to TV news editors and last to the families concerned? In these circumstances, the communication charade has a bitterness etched in misery and hardship and no one seems to care.

The International Perspective

To hear an American public relations director speak in a foreign language is a rarity even at this time of vastly expanding global business operations.

There are exceptions. Let's name some names. Heidi Looser, Deere & Company director of overseas public relations, is a Swiss national with great skill who is fluent in about four languages. To us, Looser is a fine example of a communications professional who exemplifies what is required to practice the craft globally. Deere has manufacturing plants in Canada, France, Germany, Spain, South Africa, and Argentina, and associated and joint venture companies in Turkey, Mexico, Australia, and Brazil.

Heidi Looser works to localize the company's public relations program internationally and in each country uses a tailor-made approach catering to the national tastes, local customs, languages, and the work ethic and behavioral patterns that are natural and customary for the 11,000 Deere employees in overseas facilities as well as the company's customers. Her boss, Chester K. Lasell, vice president–corporate communications, at Deere headquarters in Moline, Illinois, does the same for the 50,000 U.S. employees. There is thus a congruity in Deere communications that "fits" and is the hallmark of the Deere way of doing things fostered for nearly three decades under the leadership of the man at the top, William A. Hewitt, who retired in 1982.

We have found people like Roy J. Leffingwell, in Honolulu, formerly public relations director, Hawaiian Sugar Planters Association, to be capable in world communication. Now a public relations counselor, he knows intimately how to communicate in the Philippines, Hong Kong, Malaysia, and Australia, as well as on the U.S. mainland. Dennis H. Buckle in London was public relations adviser to the Board, UAC International Limited, a giant retailing and merchandising company operating in Africa. His company is sensitive to local issues, customs, and folkways and operates exclusively through native employees. Communications are always attuned to the receivers' needs—do not push British mannerisms and thinking down unwilling audiences' throats. Result: broadening sales, sound business relationships, and earnings on an ascending scale.

Many of our colleagues on the Continent seem to be especially good at being in tune with the other person's needs and interests and designing communications programs that are precisely synchronized to national interests and tastes. Max C. Beauchez, a veteran public relations counselor based in The Hague, is our nominee for a corporate communicator who also is a man for all seasons in Europe. He formerly worked for the Foreign Information Division, Ministry of Foreign Affairs, in the Dutch government. Beauchez reflects the Dutch business community's centuries-old ability to think and do business globally. He also has the professional communicator's learned talents to understand and respect the audiences in each country in which his programs are launched.

These international practitioners have common bonds of professionalism. All happen to be members of the International Public Relations Association, formed in 1955 and representing 50 nations. Its members are guided by the "Code of Athens," an international code of ethics. It is modeled after the United Nations Declaration of Human Rights. Such men and women guard fiercely the truth-telling process that lies at the heart of their daily work in service to their companies and to the audiences they reach. Also working on a worldwide basis are the 10,000 members in 44 countries of the growing International Association of Business Communicators. IABC's approach is that the communication process is a management problem-solving tool. Applying this reasoning broadly in business has enabled IABC to more than double its membership since 1978.

In the area of earning a seat in the council chambers of top management, an increasing number of European practitioners are already there, while in the United States one still finds the same old hackneyed yearnings to be listened to by the chairman that were voiced over 25 years ago. America's corporate communications professionals are being given a run for their money by their overseas counterparts. As Mercedes automobiles and Volvos and Toyotas are fighting their way into ascendancy in U.S. markets, so too are their corporate communications professionals gaining stature and expertise and outdistancing their Yankee mentors.

Are CEOs Afraid of Truth?

Much of the responsibility for the low quality of corporate communication today and the widening credibility gap in the corporate suites of American business lies on the mahogany desk of CEOs who still have not made the commitment to telling the truth. Yet it is impossible to pick up a business journal or a serious publication commenting on corporate life without finding an article quoting some CEO on the importance of good communication.

This charade is one of several reasons why the Japanese auto manufacturers have taken 25 percent of Detroit's market in 1982 and Congress is now flirting with the risky policy of establishing restrictive tariffs on auto imports.

So too, CEOs' unwillingness to talk clearly and honestly with constituencies is the basis for the bad feelings that have been growing between America's corporate leadership and the media. A 1981 study conducted by the American Management Association showed that 36 percent of business journalists think business executives often lie to reporters. Of business executives polled in this study, 71 percent considered themselves to be "usually accessible" to the media, but only 27 percent of the reporters thought executives this easy to reach. Nearly 73 percent of the executives responding to the poll believed that fewer than half of the reporters understood the subjects they were writing about. As a final disheartening fillip to this study, 6 percent of the business public relations directors said reporters are "dishonest about their intentions when interviewing business people," and 14 percent of the reporters agreed.[9]

Dr. Dietrich L. Leonhard, an authority on marketing research, has another dimension to add to management's communications charade: "Advertisers often do not know how to talk to people, because they do not understand people and how they really regard products."[10] He argues that all too many of the advertising studies conducted rarely prove anything except that people read magazines and newspapers, listen to radio, and watch television. Too much advertising is done for its own sake alone, with the advertisers in the dark about what they are really saying and to whom and for what. Leonhard also stresses that substantive marketing research is critically important to understanding the corporate image and the product image before much can be done to effectively change them. Madison Avenue "nose-counting" nonresearch only perpetuates the charade.

What do most corporate executives have to do to communicate sensibly and effectively and to achieve the desired understanding with their business constituencies?

The CEO—and others at the top—must commit to a corporate policy of truth telling. They must muster resources for good communication and put solid muscle into the company's efforts to interpret positions on issues vital to employees, shareholders, customers, and the rapidly proliferating regulatory agencies.

The essential reason the public often does not believe what business is saying is that business leaders themselves have created a credibility gap. Chief executive officers who profess to commit to good communication but then undermine the efforts of their communications officers to tell the truth about corporate affairs are playing in a game in which everybody loses. Washington's consumer groups and special-interest mini-conglomerates are clobbering business leaders who don't yet know how to face up to Mike Wallace's "Sixty Minutes" grueling on-camera interviews.

Simple exercises in TV on-camera skills are not the answer. Today's CEOs have to learn how to think fast on their feet, to properly—but politely—stand up to the one-share zealot at the annual meeting. But most of all, they must provide the leadership for an honest exercise in truth telling that will earn supporters for the corporation and thereby gain a competitive edge in selling products and ideas.

Rickover's Wisdom

Consider the wisdom on the subject of the charade in corporate and governmental leadership communication of Admiral Hyman G. Rickover, 82, the Navy's Chief Nuclear Officer, who has served under 13 Presidents:

> A President will never hear the truth again. Everybody in high places stands in a room full of mirrors and sees himself multiplied by servile reflections. The Oval Office can easily become such a room. . . .
>
> The United States, through Congress and through some Government officials, is being influenced by big business to a greater extent than ever before in our history. This is done through extensive and increasing lobbying, and by various types of contributions and campaign funds. It is important that appropriate legislation be enacted to limit this.
>
> Those at the head of Government departments, and their subordinates, can reach fantastic heights of hallucination. They have been encouraged by the almost universal acquiescence of ordinary people, whose penchant for self-deception is great and deep. Government officials and military officers—particularly the higher ones—are prone to vocational inflation and self-deception.[11]

Yale's brilliantly articulate President A. Bartlett Giamatti, in a now famous address to the incoming class of 1984, said:

> America is a religious nation without a coherent creed, a believing people hungering for a faith to which to give its assent. So much of what passes for moral certitude today covers a void but does not fill it. The void remains. But that is not yet the Apocalypse. Divisions and problems there are. But Armageddon is not yet. The race has a

long, long way to go. What seems exhausted to many is not; it is
they who are tired. The frenzy that sees the end at every moment
sees an illusion.

My message is simple: So much of what is heard today springs
from a fatigue and failure of nerve that would ensnare individuals
and their strength in its weakness. Beware it; do not be charmed by
it. Do not become one of those who has only the courage of other
people's convictions. Be one of those who believes in what Shakespeare
called the pauser, reason. Be one of whom coercion of any kind, whether
coercion based on race or sex or religious or political belief, is an
anathema. Leave the apocalyptic style to those who cannot, or do
not want to, do the deeply human work of finding their own voices
in the common chorus.[12]

Let us replace with honesty the charades of illusion cast in
half truths and fleshed with blurred distortions of fact. Business
executives need only revert to fundamental truth telling. When
America's business leadership learns to speak with the common
language of truth, all of its vital constituencies will listen. Hearing
truth well told and gradually recognizing consistency in corporate
and business communication, will again bring credibility back to
the boardroom, the plant bulletin board, the marketplace, and the
media.

CHAPTER 7

The Myth of the New Communication Technology

Speech is civilization itself. The word, even the most contra-dictory word, preserves contact—it is silence which isolates.

Thomas Mann

BUSINESS EXECUTIVES fell in love with the computer in the 1950s, insisting their company had to have one to stay ahead in the technology game, and this history is now repeating itself in the arena of communication hardware. This is the era of multi-image slide shows, high-decibel sound tracks, and wide-screen images that invade the senses (and sometimes stampede the sensibilities) of top executives forced to sit through interminable hours of presentations being passed off as "communication."

Too many American business executives have swallowed whole the presumption that if an electric typewriter is good, then a word processor is better. "Bigger, faster, more complex is better" is the way the litany goes.

We can think of a half-dozen large public relations firms, themselves owned by advertising agencies, whose key decision makers think that the only way to present their credentials as counselors in communication to CEOs is to inflict on them a 20-minute multi-image, fast-paced slide show of their professional expertise. While this bewildering multiplicity of images is churned onto a screen from a whirling dervish of a slide projector, demonstrating only technical prowess with 35-mm slides, it communicates little about brain power. Such imagery is no substitute for the firsthand understanding of the consumer's changing needs, and treads heavy-handed through a forest of clichés and hyperbole that merely lumps together all the public relation firms as slide-show presenters using identical hardware, being wedded to the frozen images of stock slides.

From the perspective of the busy CEO, the view is of one slide show competing with six other slide shows. Seldom do we see counselors and consultants reaching the management decision makers with messages that are low-key, readily understandable, and persuasive and that address the specific needs and concerns of the individual executive and his unique company situation.

To hold the attention of senior management decision makers requires a healthy amount of authentic research, honest fact finding, and first-hand field investigation.

There is another way to talk with management. Several years ago we were invited to advise a multi-billion-dollar merchandising corporation that was approaching a major acquisition. The CEO and CFO were anxious to get their story told and understood in the financial community. Our thinking was that we ought to quietly visit with a half-dozen well-positioned security analysts and get their views on the company and management's underlying strategy and their perception of the securities and the future. The perspective of the men and women on the Street whose professional judgments govern the buy-or-sell decisions of the legions of brokers trading the stock was the focal point in the opinion-shaping process.

In about four days we had taken the pulse of the Street. We submitted a summary that included the exact language of analysts and astute investment bankers. Field interviewing invitably tells you *what* is going on, but if you dig deep enough and ask the right questions of the right sources, you can zero in on the nerve endings and also find out *why* the market is behaving the way it is.

We added a few visual aids, using as a model the Sunday business section of the *New York Times,* which tends to use graphics that are imaginative and simple.

That's the way most managers we know like to receive information and briefing data.

The new hardware never creates any ideas or generates any plans. Only thoughtful interpretation can do that, and *that* is the key ingredient to the effective use of any technological instrument of communication. Infatuation with multi-images and expensive communication hardware is growing at a pace that threatens to destroy creativity. It undermines the very purpose of communication as it relates to reason, thoughtful responses, and the individual human needs of the people who are customers, stockholders, voters, and taxpayers.

Machine No-Think

Even though today's fastest computers can be programmed to do extraordinary things (for example, the Japanese efforts to create software to translate Chinese scientific and technical language into English), the fact remains that machines don't think. The human mind is the most magnificent computer in the world. It will never be replaced by any form of hardware or technology, no matter how sophisticated.

This truism needs to be reexamined by the legions of people in business who have become infatuated with the new hardware, such as the video technology that permits meetings to be transmitted over great distances by satellite communication and by long-distance telephone lines. As business travel becomes more expensive, it is certainly logical to consider spanning the distance electronically. Such methods can be time savers, can trim budgets, and perform many useful purposes in communication, training, and education.

But the danger we see with the flood of equipment coming on the market and with middle managers and communication directors falling in love with it is that the fundamental importance of original thought, reflection, and dialogue are diminished. Sound management planning and strategically developed ideas that hew closely to senior management's best planning are in danger of being eroded. Distortion and distance are thus growing between the quality of the thinking produced at the top of the corporate structure and what passes for communication when it reaches the action level at the other end of the corporate communication pipeline. This is a dangerous trend. We believe that infatuation with the new communication hardware is robbing the spirit of excellence that should consistently be built into all management communication.

Some of the worst offenders, of course, are advertising agencies whose staff people and account executives think that to bedazzle the client is commensurate with demonstrating creative thinking and imaginative solutions to complex marketing, public opinion, or attitude problems. We have heard for many years the oft-repeated definition of good advertising being salesmanship in print, or salesmanship on television, or salesmanship on radio. Indeed, good advertising thoughtfully researched and imaginatively written to meet the true marketing and sales requirements of a client is a useful and valuable business tool. But to assume advertising techniques are appropriate tools for communicating management's messages to the whole corporation, or even to some of its important constituencies, is a case of a method being applied in an inappropriate setting for the wrong reasons.

Seduced by computer technology that promises "good human engineering," many companies have converted important human messages to customers, employees, suppliers, and even special business friends into computer-generated modes of communication. These are often dull and insulting to the receiver's intelligence. Such messages are easily distorted, and stultify the honesty and validity of messages best transmitted by other people.

We can recall the power and the forceful impression cast by optimum communication requiring no technology whatsoever. The scene is a classroom where a knowledgeable and caring teacher is simply talking with a group of students. The most complex instrument of communication technology needed is a piece of chalk and a blackboard.

The interplay of a fine mind reaching out and communicating, touching other minds with messages of importance, is powerful. This form of communication fosters credibility. It is a model for effective business communication.

Another means of reaching minds and involving employees in the communication process does use the most sophisticated video hardware but in a sensitive and caring way to preserve the personal touch. C. James Jensen is chairman and CEO of Thousand Trails, Inc., in Seattle. His company is young and growing fast in one of the new expanding service industries of tomorrow. It owns and operates private membership campgrounds on the West Coast, in Texas, and in British Columbia.

"Our management objective is to provide our people with an atmosphere in which to grow. As we grow bigger, our challenge is to bring our people closer together," Jensen says.[1]

We have 800 full-time employees and 1,000 including part-timers during our summer peak periods. They are spread over 21 locations in five states and in Canada. Other members of management and I communicate with them through a video network we have created, and in effect, we have gone into the television production business as the best way to reach our people.

Every two weeks we produce a 15-minute to a 30-minute TV program, "Insights." We communicate with our people directly by this medium. Every effort is made to focus on individual employees and to give them an opportunity to participate in the preparation of Insights and share their thoughts and ideas. Our camera crew spends 80 percent of its time in the field. I guess we have about $250,000 invested in the equipment and hardware, but it has literally made millions for us. We like to deal in a visual mode rather than auditory as is the mode for written memorandums. Using video, I know our messages are constructed the right way and there is no distortion in the process of transmission. But we don't rely on video alone. We use "Open Forum," regular employee group meetings where I and all in management meet face to face with our employees and we encourage a vigorous give-and-take dialogue. I want to hear how they feel, and then I want to respond right then and there.[2]

Does it work? You bet. For fiscal 1982, Jensen's company is reporting doubled earnings over 1981—exceeding $7 million in net earnings versus $3.3 million for the prior year, based on a 40 percent increase in sales to $56 million—a record high. But it's work. Jensen says he spends 80 percent of his personal work time on all forms of communication.

People Talking with People

People talking with people is still the vital link for business, at all levels of the organization. When businesses were small in America, the owner/manager had an intimate sense of how best to serve customers. Audio processors, telecommunications, satellite transmission of pictures and words, and the opportunity for two-way televised interaction with vast audiences have stimulated the substitution of robots of information for personal communication from the CEO. Truthful, congruent messages from the top are still the best way to communicate with customers, stockholders, and employees with feelings and needs. In the last analysis, it is they who are the real owners of our businesses and the source of corporate power in the United States.

Nothing has come close to replacing the value of the spoken

word—especially coming personally from a corporate leader. All the fancy communications hardware in the world can never substitute for the positive benefit of interpersonal communication between boss and subordinate, board member and manager. Or between co-workers.

Personal communication is hard work. The easy way out for many executives is to hide themselves behind the new communication hardware assuming that the technology is helping take care of communication. As we have argued in Part One, of all the many factors that may contribute to a fulfilling and meaningful work experience—salary and fringe benefits, working conditions, co-worker relations, environmental conditions, the work itself—American workers say the one that really counts is a positive view of top management.

If senior management will use a research base in the communication process, executives can learn to formulate messages to employees and other key constituencies that address the real issues of genuine concern. The machinery of communication in today's world is more than adequate. A good case could be made that the machinery is already overdeveloped, a threatening mechanism driving out intellect. What we want to see are managers who will commit funds and energy and top attention to fathoming the underlying causes of disquiet, unease, and mistrust that are undermining the role of leadership.

American corporations are accustomed to spending vast sums on product research, engineering research, and research for improved packaging. How about an equal measure of commitment to the uses of research in the social and behavioral sciences to aid the overall communication process in business and industry? We must devote more of our resources to the task of finding out how best to transmit the ideas and creative thought processes that eventually will produce the behavior modification necessary for lasting success in corporate America.[3]

The distinguished sociologist Alfred McLung Lee, past president of the American Sociological Association, argued passionately 40 years ago for emphasis in research and study on the application of the social sciences to business and society's needs for conflict resolution. He equates "public relations specialist" with "societal technician," an approach which comes very close to clinical sociology. Recently, he has renewed his argument:

Now that human society faces the greatest threats to its persistence that it ever has—threats that are bringing crises to individuals and to organizations of all sorts—all possible technologies are being tried as ways of coping. Unfortunately, these ways include irrational, mystical, and delusionary ones, ones that are misleadingly manipulative as well as ones that have some chance of being helpful and socially constructive.

This growing crisis in European-American affairs represents a tremendous challenge to clinical sociologists as well as to many other specialists and generalists. Let us hope that we shall have increasing opportunities to demonstrate and improve the usefulness of our diagnoses, therapies, and strategies and that, thus, they will come to be more and more widely employed.[4]

By whatever name we choose to characterize the managers or the consultants who must deal in the realities of interpersonal behavior in business, industry, government, and society at large, there is a common bond to all their endeavors. They must communicate to others the essence of the social or industrial process. That requires teamwork, cooperation, mutual understanding. It is an *intellectual* function not substantially aided by gears, motors, chips, or electronic circuits. Human brain power is the persuading element in cultivating loyalty, honesty and open expression, and the shared feelings and beliefs so vital to harmonious business relationships. America's new communication technology, while useful in processing messages, is no substitute for the human quality of the content in messages from the people at the top.

Enemies to this process of truthful and sensible communication are the pressures of life at the top, persistent demands on the time of the CEO, and, unfortunately, sometimes the impact of industrial-engineering—oriented consultants who preach too hard the time-saving and energy-saving benefits of hardware aimed at stretching the impact and influence of the CEO. The consequent result of undue reliance on the sophisticated and cold hardware of modern electronic communication is isolation of the CEO and dangerous distancing between the leader and the constituencies—the people—whose feelings, emotions, and reason must be appealed to.

If today's CEOs will work at the task of being good personal communicators in their own right and resist the temptation of electronic crutches, the benefits will be evident in manifold ways which will fall to the bottom line.

Human Robotics

Today the hottest prospect for a big salary in the writing profession is the treasured post of speech writer to the CEO. Some companies, among them the cash-rich oil companies and the utilities, are paying $100,000 to $150,000 a year for smooth scribes to craft the polished words the CEO will read, well rehearsed by his speech trainer, to a presumably enthralled audience.

We think CEOs worth their salt should be skilled and articulate enough to be able to say it on their own. We would not deny access to staff support for business executives in this area, but the danger zone has been crossed when the speech writer begins to do the *thinking* for the inarticulate CEO. Men and women at the top cannot abdicate the role of top management responsibility for good communication to a scribe-for-hire. No one can do the thinking for the CEO.

Many corporations dealing directly with consumers now have "Departments of Customer Relations" and consumer relations specialists whose job it is supposedly to communicate with consumers when they have problems or needs that are not being met by the product or service. What started out as a sound idea has too often degenerated into a game called "Protect the Business." The reality of life at this moment is that if a customer has a legitimate complaint, it is nearly impossible to communicate with someone at the top. Platoons of underlings provide formidable barriers around chief executives who are no longer in touch with the people who are their consumers.

In an age of conjured visual images and manipulative behavior, the essence of the American Republic still rests firmly on the Founding Fathers' principle of a well-informed populace. No better authority on the power and the value of old-fashioned honest communication is available than from the wise words of the lanky lawyer from Illinois:

> In this and like communities public sentiment is everything. With public sentiment nothing can fail; without it nothing can succeed; consequently he who molds public sentiment goes deeper than he who enacts statutes or pronounces decisions. He makes statutes and decisions possible or impossible to be executed.[5]

Like the Surgeon General's warning, that historic message might well be imprinted on every new piece of communication hardware installed throughout corporate America.

PART THREE

Back to Basics

CHAPTER 8

The Communication Audit— Company Communication on the Psychiatric Couch

Nothing astonishes men so much as common sense and plain dealing.

Ralph Waldo Emerson

THE SCENE IS a large, abandoned office formerly used as a secretarial pool area in the days before the company headquarters was moved to a new building in an expensive corporate development in the suburbs. All the furniture and window coverings have been removed and the electricity turned off in most of the inner office areas. Folding chairs have been brought into the room and set in a semicircle off to one corner. A large coffee pot, stacks of Styrofoam cups, and a box of sweet rolls have been provided by the company.

Our 12 guests will be arriving any minute. For the moment, the room is completely quiet except for the rhythmic mechanical hum from one of the vintage machines in the factory directly below us. It is June in Kansas City, and outside it is raining heavily.

Our client company is a 60-year-old, $55 million manufacturer of electrical wiring harnesses, primarily for the automotive industry, with other products serving trucking, farm equipment, heavy industrial equipment, and the construction industries. It is operating in the red, badly in need of diversification, and searching for ways to respond to an angry and demoralized workforce. Employee job satisfaction is exceptionally low due in large part to management's emergency action to eliminate the company-paid pension program in order to strengthen the firm's weakened cash position. Because an effective internal communication system did not exist at a time when it was especially needed, many employees first heard about the demise of their pension program through the local media.

For the next two and one-half hours we will talk with and listen to our third employee group that day, all workers from the old factory below us, as part of a Communication Audit we are conducting for the company. This particular group of 12 men and women is one that we will always remember as an example of the profound value that can be gained from simply listening to people. It also stands to remind us of the many times we have been personally touched by people's willingness to try and their basic goodness, even in the face of bitter disillusionment.

Two of our 12 interviewees are hearing-impaired. They are men who work the powerful wire-drawing machines, so noisy that by company tradition only deaf people are hired to operate them. An interpreter in American Sign Language has been brought in for this meeting, but this pair of veteran workers often seem to be a few sentences ahead of her. They communicate rapidly, signing to each other, nodding their heads, sometimes slapping their knees for emphasis. Thirty minutes into the session, after we have made brief opening comments and offered a few probing questions, the energy level in the room begins to rise. Small talk is over. The group dynamic swells into a skyrocketing array of verbal and non-verbal communication. Employees have so much they want to say if they sense somebody is genuinely listening.

Months later, we find ourselves in a completely different physical setting in the East Coast corporate corridor between New York City and Philadelphia. In a plush woodgrained and leather-appointed executive conference room, we sit with five upper-level executives from a division of one of the world's largest corporations.

Total revenues for the year were $59 billion, net income $6.9 billion. Over decades of sustained growth, the corporation had become "overmanaged" with a glut of white-collar, college-educated executives stuck in middle-level jobs with little authority and no chance for advancement. Top management has initiated a program to delete one or more of these middle levels, creating tremors of fear and insecurity throughout the middle management ranks.

The five executives around our conference table represent one of these middle management levels, a likely candidate for elimination. Their futures are uncertain. All earn six-figure incomes with outstanding fringe benefits. One sits with his arms crossed tightly. Two of them are leaning back into soft chairs with their feet on the table, hands interlaced behind their heads. The other three are leaning forward in their chairs, eager to begin.

Two hours later, ties are loosened, shirt sleeves rolled up, and the entire atmosphere in the room has become warm, cordial, and open. In a small, subtle and revealing way, this group interview session has marked the beginning of a process to improve the quality of work life (QWL) for the professional people who work in this plush corporate division. The problem, though not yet solved, is now at least something they have begun to deal with directly and honestly.

What we are describing here are Depth Interviews, part of a process we use in our Communication Audit.

Untying the Gordian Knot

A frustrating problem in dealing with the concept of communication, particularly for those practical-minded managers who are by nature suspicious of the social sciences in the first place, is that the word "communication" is ubiquitous. Simple definitions of the term won't suffice.

Communication has inherent social relevance. Any area of concern to the human condition can be linked to communication. If communication includes the total exchange of information, written and oral, nonverbal, involving machines as well as people, then how do we deal with a subject that includes everything?

Let's make some sense of our use of the word "communication" by assigning it a meaningful location in the organizational scheme of things. Figure 8.1 provides a basic illustration of what has been called the Organizational Causal Sequence.[1] It is a cause-and-effect model that provides a clearer view of the role of communication in the organization.

Reading from left to right on Figure 8.1, we see that there are certain external and internal causal factors, the latter being under the direct control of management, which have an impact

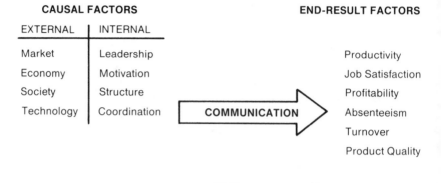

FIGURE 8.1   Organizational Causal Sequence

on the organization. On the right side are the end-result factors, measures of organizational performance. Communication is the critical linkage between these causes and end results. Everything that occurs between the time a causal factor is first felt in an organization and the time when its impact begins to show up in results is reflected in the organization's communication system. Regardless of where the problem initiates—in marketing, sales, finance, engineering, industrial relations, accounting—its presence will show up in the communication system. Any event or condition that will eventually influence results will be detectable in the organization's communication apparatus if we are sensitive to it—if somebody is listening. In essence, communication is an early warning system allowing us to infer what is about to happen.

Communication is the business organization's lifeblood. An examination of an organization's communication system by specialists armed with the proper tools and know-how can provide a whole body scan of organizational health.

Our Communication Audit involves a three-pronged strategy for tapping into the organization's communication system to take a reading on the rich information it holds. This technique, modified and shaped by us over years of practice, has proven to be an effective way of capturing the real corporate dynamic underlying several layers of superficial protective barriers. For a number of good reasons, the technique works powerfully. First, let us describe the three parts of the Communication Audit: Depth Interviewing, the Attitude Barometer, and Artifact Analysis.

Part One—Depth Interviewing

Depth Interviewing relies heavily on old-fashioned, face-to-face meetings. By talking with and listening to enough people first-hand, genuine insights can be gained into the internal and external communication system of the organization. This is not unlike a seasoned physician talking with a patient to probe and identify physical symptoms.

To help bring into focus one mechanism of this interviewing process, we would ask business leaders this question: "When was the last time you sat down and listened for two and one-half hours to what one or more of your employees had on his or her mind?" For most business leaders the answer is "Not in living memory."

This technique couples the investigative reporting of journalism with the subtleties of psychiatric nondirective interviewing. This method of active listening is not new. Its use in industry was initiated in Cicero, Illinois, at Western Electric's Hawthorne Works in the early 1930s. Perhaps the most lasting and useful finding of the famous Hawthorne Studies was the measurable value of the unstructured interview in the work setting.[2] While the conduct of such interviews requires considerable skill and experience with the method, its use in the business setting has led to bountiful results.

Such Depth Interviews require a two-to-three-month effort, usually with a team of two interviewers and involve about 150 employees. Workers are interviewed singly, in pairs, and in small groups of five to twelve. These are not "focus group" interviews in the popular sense of the term. They are not gripe sessions. And there is nothing touchy-feely about them à la the California fad approach to counseling or group therapy. They derive from the studies of the Group Dynamic process stemming from the research of topological psychologist Kurt Lewin in the 1930s and the 1940s at the University of Iowa and later at Massachusetts Institute of Technology.[3]

All interviewees are assured strict anonymity. The atmosphere is informal and open. Uninhibited communication is encouraged. Our intent is to have all participants feel free and protected in sharing their innermost thoughts, emotions, and, most important, their constructive ideas for improving work and the work environment. Deliberate effort is made to remove all possible barriers to open communication. The interviews are not recorded. Notes taken by the interviewers are open for inspection by the participants. When a small group is being interviewed, the seating is arranged in a circle and every effort is made to engage in dialogue in a genuinely democratic manner with conscious effort given to courtesy and respect for each worker—no matter what his or her job, length of service, or background. These interviews run from one to two and one-half hours, during which time we interweave a few standardized questions (such as "On a scale of 1 to 10, 1 being poor and 10 being excellent, how would you rate your morale?"), enabling us to cross-check information and map trends.

Interviews done in this mode are exhausting work. Actively listening, communicating genuine concern and sincerity to an initially skeptical audience, requires a great deal from the interviewer. Sincerity cannot be play-acted or faked. Once the interviewees sense the session is for real, and this often requires the entire first hour of the interview, they begin to place trust in the process. The dialogue is usually salty, honest, and real. Sometimes smouldering anger bursts into flame. Fists pound tables, cigarettes are nervously lit and snuffed out. Some give vent to tears. Often, disagreements are brought into the open. The air crackles with tension—and relief. Emotions are expressed; deep-seated feelings are brought to the surface.

Part Two—Attitude Barometer*

The second key element of the Communication Audit is a measurement device we call the Attitude Barometer, sample questions of which are provided below:

SAMPLE BAROMETER QUESTIONS

In your dealings with people at other levels in the company, you are treated courteously.

( )	( )	( )	( )	( )	( )	( )	( )	( )	( )
1	2	3	4	5	6	7	8	9	10

| Strongly disagree | Disagree | Neither agree nor disagree | Agree | Strongly agree |

Over the last few months, how would you rate the honesty of communication between you and your immediate supervisor?

( )   ( )   ( )   ( )   ( )   ( )   ( )   ( )   ( )   ( )
 1   2   3   4   5   6   7   8   9   10

The worst   Getting   About the   Getting   The best
                 worse   same   better

How would you rate your confidence in top management?

( )   ( )   ( )   ( )   ( )   ( )   ( )   ( )   ( )   ( )
 1   2   3   4   5   6   7   8   9   10

   Poor   Fair   Average   Good   Excellent

The Barometer is an unassuming 10-to-12-item questionnaire that enables the measurement of change in attitudes over time through readministration three or four times annually. All employees, from the CEO on down, fill out the Barometer. The questions themselves are different from company to company, having grown out of the pattern of human responses culled from the cumulative Depth Interviews. The Barometer is easy and simple to fill out, requiring only a few minutes. It is also carefully structured not to raise false expectations in the respondents. It promises no miracles, only the beginning of an active change process with the respondents themselves becoming the change agents. It is genuinely participative.

Many companies misuse questionnaires, and a number of well-meaning but unenlightened management consultants must take a large share of the blame. This misuse may occasionally take the form of an improperly designed questionnaire, inappropriate statistical analysis of the responses, or faulty computing of the responses in order to elicit an overall "score" from a set of questions. When spotted, these problems are relatively easy to correct. A skilled manager properly trained in survey research can guard against them in the first place. But there is a worse, far more common problem: establishing inappropriate objectives for the use of a questionnaire and thereby using the data to answer the wrong questions.

Questionnaires are simply not effective instruments for answering the vital "why" questions having to do with attitudes. All too often, they are misused this way. A questionnaire can tell you *what* people are feeling about a certain issue, but it just can't get at the *why* behind those feelings. The why is always going to be more complex, relating to events and situations in the past and anticipated in the future. Such information cannot be accurately captured by checking a box on a questionnaire.

When a questionnaire is used for this purpose, the result is a set of numbers, usually percentages, that gloss over the real issues because the vast and rich information available in nonverbal communication and the "third language" of group dynamics can't be measured by administering a questionnaire. If you want to know the why, there is no substitute for talking with and listening to people. The real value of questionnaire data—and this is exclusively how we use our Barometer—is to track changes in *what* people are feeling and reacting to over a period of time. Documenting this attitude change is essential to knowing whether things are getting better, getting worse, or staying the same. But to find out *why,* we have to interact with people in the more meaningful setting of the Depth Interviews.

Responses to the simple but far-reaching Barometer questions provide quantitative information that is essential to properly diagnosing the ills and strengths of a company's communication system when combined with the qualitative insights gained through the Depth Interviews. Combining these two very different and complementary analytic techniques yields a precise, reliable examination that not only composes an accurate picture of company communication but captures the true feelings and thinking of the employees representing the dynamic of the workforce, plus the good ideas of the company's own people. This technique of combining quantitative and qualitative information increases the validity and the value of the data. We employ our own computer program and analytic technique for tracking changes in attitudes over time through repeated Barometer readings and follow-up interviews.

Part Three—Artifact Analysis

The third dimension of the Communication Audit process is a thoroughgoing review of all existing systems, records, and devices of corporate communication. We study two or three years of annual and quarterly financial reports, employee newsletters, company magazines, president's letters, bulletin-board announcements, memoranda, company general orders, and policy bulletins and a host of widely differing forms of written communication. To examine oral and interpersonal communication, we also review video tapes of meetings and conferences and the minutes of committee meetings and study the style and content of management's regular patterns of behavior in dealing with people person to person. Some companies use public audio announcements, closed-circuit TV, and other audio-visual techniques. These too are studied. Then the effectiveness of *all* the ongoing communications is weighed and evaluated in terms of the results being achieved, which will, in part, show up in the findings of the Barometer readings and from the Depth Interviews.

We have seen companies spend millions of dollars on expensive corporate advertising and elaborate publications that miss the mark, often bouncing off the thick skins and protective barriers of the audience like BB pellets on armor plate. And we have seen companies consistently spending such vast sums without relying on any sensible method for measuring or researching their messages' impact and overall effectiveness. Seldom do we find management endeavoring to study critically and to render good business judgments about the wisdom of these substantial expenditures. Let's examine this point more closely.

An indication of how wasteful some phases of corporate communication are today can be gained from a survey we conducted in 1980 on the cost of producing corporate annual reports. Having counseled CEOs and chief financial officers for years on how best to talk to the financial community and shareholders through the annual report, we decided to find out the real cost of annual reports.

This study was prompted by L. Chandler Smith, chairman and chief executive officer of Conchemco, Incorporated, a medium-size industrial company based in the Kansas City area. Smith wanted to know if his costs on the annual report were in line with other companies and what was a reasonable amount to budget for a modern, well-designed pictorial report. When we checked the literature of U.S. business, there was surprisingly little precise information on annual-report costs to be found.

We designed a survey questionnaire and sent it to the CFOs of 100 Fortune 500 companies whose annual reports and full-disclosure procedures put them in the forefront of the best in the nation. We deliberately by-passed the corporate communication people, feeling that the financial officer would be more direct and open about yielding a true picture of actual costs. We wanted no one's apple to be polished, and we said so.

Our responses came quickly. It was like touching a raw nerve ending. We sensed in the replies a collective sigh of relief that someone finally was probing this sensitive area of executive office budgeting. Twenty-five corporations responded to the 22-item questionnaire, which deliberately provided ample room for off-the-cuff commentary. Amazingly, we found that no one was keeping track of the amount of executive time spent on the annual report, one of the most important printed communication documents of a corporate organization. We asked for "guesstimates" of senior-officer time spent and the cost of that time, and found that the average senior management time spent on the report was 1,000 hours. Average cost of that time figured out to about $275 per hour.

Thus over a quarter of a million dollars was committed to the report by senior officers, yet no accounting of that time appeared in the budgetary or per copy costs of the reports! When we asked how the report was measured for performance against objectives, we found none of the respondent companies had a formalized research program to assess its effectiveness.

Only four companies made any effort to measure results via even informal research. All tended to watch their competitors' reports and listen to informal playback from shareholders, analysts, and employees, but none had advanced to the point where a formal effort was conducted to double-check these sizable expenditures using established research procedures. Our study showed that in press runs under 100,000 copies the average cost of the report was $2.50. Over 100,000 copies ran $1.40 each. (These figures represent only supplier services such as printing, art, design, and photography and are for 1980.)

For another view of the true cost of the annual report, we penetrated the ranks of upper management and found a "seat-of-the-pants" approach to measurement. Even here, no efforts were apparently being made to account for that precious officer time, one of the most expensive parts of the corporate communication process. Little wonder there is a need at the top for a more systematic and sensible accounting of corporate resources assigned to this vital stewardship function.

The companies participating in this study that gave us permission to use their names along with the findings were International Paper, Bendix, Rockwell International, General Foods, and ConAgra—a small but telling tribute to managers gutsy enough to speak the truth.

One astute director of financial planning wrote us:

Annual reports by and large are excellent analyses of the accounting model of a company. But very few give a good analysis of the true economic model of the firm. And sadly, if you want to try to do anything toward answering that question you have to fight with the lawyers and accountants. Many companies won't bother.

Our survey uncovered some sensitive areas in revealing the hidden costs of annual reports, and the *Wall Street Journal* ran a page 1 summary of our findings on February 26, 1980. We received mail and inquiries from all over the United States and from internationally based companies; but our hunch is that little authentic research on annual-report effectiveness has been launched since.

What the Audit Reveals

Our three components of the Communication Audit combine to provide a sensitive investigative tool for tapping into the storehouse of valuable and usable information available in the company's communication system. The Audit provides a laboratory analysis of organizational health by listening to the corporate heartbeat—the workforce.

Armed with this information, management is then able to make sensible decisions about changes needed to improve work attitudes and management effectiveness and generally make a measurable contribution to organizational performance. Follow-up Barometer readings will tell just how much improvement people say is actually taking place, and periodic Depth Interviews will enable reexamination of the substantive issues—the why—behind these trends.

Summary findings of an initial Communication Audit are sometimes startling, are always informative, and cannot easily be ignored. Over the years, our Audit reports and recommendations to management have varied widely from company to company and industry to industry. The Audit findings have often fueled a change in management philosophy and have, on occasion, even led to replacing the CEO. Information gathered through the Audit process can be powerful stuff.

In one recent case, the findings of the Audit culminated in a Communication Workshop we designed to involve senior management and members of the board of directors of one company. During this day-and-a-half, off-site workshop, the board members were given a novel opportunity to participate meaningfully in setting a course for the future of this company. At one point, a group of foremen and plant supervisors were brought into the proceedings to interact directly with senior officers and board members. This was a way of bridging the great distance between their views of what was going on in the organization and what was actually happening as the workforce experienced the reality of life in plant and office—often, two entirely different perceptions of company life. The result was a better understanding of each other's views, a clearer focus on the big picture, resolution of some deep-seated misunderstandings of roles and responsibilities, and the opportunity to get the company's people working together more harmoniously.

Some common themes run through our Communication Audit findings across companies and industries. While every situation is unique, these themes recur time and again and we have come to believe they are essential ingredients to the renaissance in American corporate leadership. They have to do with truth telling.

Sifting from numerous Audits conducted over the years and distilled from 30 years of experience with internal and external corporate audiences of widely varying types, we have been able to formulate some basic truths of good business communication. We think they apply as well in nonbusiness settings—in government, the nonprofit sector, local communities, and even family and interpersonal relationships.

We call them Ten Truisms of Corporate Communication:*

1. *Tell It Straight from the Shoulder.* Plain talk, sometimes a little colorful or a bit salty, helps to make it real, but watch out for hip-shooting and foot-in-mouth syndrome. The power of the printed word remains undiminished, so think carefully about what you want your company to say, then lay it out truthfully. Consumers and employees can sense double-talk. Talk across to your audience, never down.

2. *Be Human.* No business is perfect. It is common knowledge that each year more than 85 percent of new product introductions are failures. Your company isn't making authentic progress unless you blow one once in a while. Admit it. Shareholders and employees are human. They don't expect you to be a Superman. If you have to go back to the drawing board because the product wasn't right—tell them *how* you're making it better.

3. *Keep It Simple.* We know it's a complex world, and you may have to be an Einstein to run your company, but don't talk in jargon. There is nothing quite so potent as a clear, striking idea well written and presented in polished words.

4. *Look for the Drama.* Behind those multi-million-dollar business decisions there is enough drama and excitement for a dozen first-run Broadway hits. Dig it out with some legwork. This is part of the full package of truth telling. Let the excitement in business come through.

5. *Be a Good Listener.* Keep your nose to the grindstone but your ear to the ground. Use practical marketing research principles. Get out and talk to your customers and employees—ask them for their ideas. If you think something looks and sounds great, let your audience react to it before going into production. Then listen to what they are saying between the lines. But don't count noses. Statistics can never tell you the "why" factor. Look for *why* people are reacting as they do.

6. *Recognize Both Women and Men.* Your audience is at least half female. Your workforce, office and plant, is heavily oriented toward women employees. Almost two-thirds of the nation's assets are controlled or influenced by a woman's viewpoint.

7. *Package Your Message Attractively.* Everyone is interested in the bottom line, but plain black on white can be dull. Part of the message is the medium. Make an effort to dress up your annual or quarterly reports. Look to journalism for hints. Make your reports breathe action; show real people doing real work and identify them. Avoid design for design's sake. Keep it as fresh as today's front page. Use photography to paint with light, imaginatively. Good taste costs no more.

8. *Shorten It.* It's hard work to get to the point. But do it. Say it well, but get it across fast. Sift through to the nuggets of gold, then present the most significant things first. Keep your eye on what's important to the audience, not to you.

9. *Avoid Legalese.* Don't sell out to the lawyers. "No comment" *is* a comment and it's usually negative. The court of public opinion is more potent than statutes. Lawyers talking to

lawyers erode profits and create no new products or markets. Government agencies are proliferating in an effort to serve and protect the common people—get on their side.

10. *Saying Won't Make It So.* Truth in advertising will sell a lot more than shrill hyperbole. By all means, put your best foot forward—build a quality product that does what it is supposed to, will last, and delivers value and satisfaction. Then back your product. Tell why it's high-quality. They're listening out there, and they usually don't make the same mistake twice.

* Copyright © Ronald Goodman & Company, Inc., 1979.

How To Get Action

Back to our opening scene of the Communication Audit in the Kansas City industrial manufacturer.

Latent energy in the workers is tapped by the probing interviewing. As soon as the employees sense that the consultants have a mandate from the top to work for authentic change, powerful things begin to happen. In the group described and in others like it, the winds of change begin to blow over the course of several weeks. Minds are opened to what could happen if everyone began to pull harder—and together.

Workers know where the waste is. Long ago they gave up in silent, bitter frustration at correcting such gross abuse, having been turned off repeatedly by bureaucratic red tape and buck passing. But when they hear a rescue party chopping through the overgrowth that has been impeding the normal flow of information, they inevitably perk up.

In this Depth Interview group an energetic and bright secretary, sensing that the power of the group could initiate change and reflecting a new excitement, could stand it no longer. She asked, "What do you want us to do?"

Our answer was "You tell us."

She suggests they organize.

"Let's form a committee," someone else chimes in.

"What'll we call it?" another voice asks.

"How about the *Communication Committee?*"

The secretary pulls out a pad of paper and begins to take minutes.

One of the more voluble of the worker-talkers finds himself nominated to chair the committee. They begin making a list of areas in the plant and in their sales office where they *know* they can save time and money using their own ideas for work improvement.

"Who'll carry our messages to the top?" they ask.

"We'll help open the channel," we say as consultants.

"The CEO hired us, he'll listen to a consensus of his employees if you organize your ideas and present them clearly," we remind them.

And that's exactly what happened the day new lines of communication were born from that Audit. They are still functioning today. Several members of that Communication Committee, their department head, the plant manager, and the CEO himself have since asked, "Why didn't we do something like this before?"

CHAPTER 9

The Power of Leadership Through Human Communication

All life therefore comes back to the question of our speech, the medium through which we communicate with one another; for all life comes back to the question of our relations with one another.

Henry James

U<small>NCOUNTED NUMBERS</small> of business organizations in this country are merely muddling through. Vast numbers of American companies are barely profitable, if at all. Thousands have angry and aliented workers, laboring in aging and musty factories producing second-class products. America deserves something better.

A great company in our sense of the term is a business whose people at all levels have a clear understanding of their mission both as employees and as an organization. They know where they are heading. They understand the philosophy and basic principles that guide the enterprise. They unerringly approach their duties and interpersonal relationships with an even and steady adherence to a standard of excellence that is there by managerial design. In this type of company our analysis has almost always shown that good communication is doctrinaire. Management at all levels between the top and the bottom of the corporate structure seeks to practice a common, comfortable, easy sharing of information. The Doctrine of Open Communication is alive and well and thrives in this special atmosphere.

Open communication does not mean that everyone always speaks his or her mind or that everyone has access to the same information; nor does it mean that there is no such thing as confidentiality. Open communication should not be confused with an easy or permissive form of management. As any experienced marriage counselor might advise, openness in relationships with others is much more difficult to achieve and maintain than is being closed and secretive. It means genuine respect for the dignity of the individual. In a truly great company, customers' complaints are a serious matter. They are usually minimal, but when a complaint does occur, responsible people take action swiftly. Such a company assumes responsibility for the integrity and proper performance of its products and services and is quick and sure about its response.

Open communication means that questions are not only tolerated but encouraged even when they may be unsettling. It means that the decision-making process tends to remain "unfrozen" longer than is typical in a closed organization. At any time during the formulation or implementation of policies, members of the organization are free to say, "Wait a minute, let's reconsider this; here's why." In fact, it's considered a responsibility, not just a privilege. It also means that when questions are raised, the questioner is sure of getting a straightforward response.

At the annual meeting in such a company, the chairman does not have to routinely defer to a subordinate for an answer to a question from a shareholder or a security analyst. Probing questions from shareholders are expected at the annual meeting as everyday facts of life for management. The CEO does not have to rehearse pat or standard answers. In an atmosphere of universal appreciation and recognition of the importance of equal access to the facts, these are logical and reasonable demands. Management in such an open company recognizes that sharing information so that all concerned can achieve an intelligent understanding of the company's business operations is normal. Time and money are willingly spent to keep all constituencies well informed.

Less Said the Better

Open dissemination of information is oftentimes in conflict with the advice of legal departments, which generally seem to operate under the old-fashioned principle that the less said, the better. In fact, saying nothing often conveys the single most potent negative message that could be given.

While we wish to tilt no windmills with lawyers, we are firm in our conviction that the legal fraternity is very often out of step with the true needs of senior management operating in a real world where increasingly activist-oriented constituencies are determined to have access to and understand information affecting their lives and fortunes. Lawyers following the so-called prudent-man rule do damage to their clients under the guise of protecting the legal interests of the corporation by urging "no comment" and secrecy.

We believe that too often corporate lawyers fall into an overly influential leadership role, actually making key decisions *for* company executives rather than *with* them. An aggressive lawyer may find it relatively easy to intimidate and bewilder an unenlightened manager, with the result that the entire management function becomes confused with the legal considerations that are but one of its aspects. When asked, most seasoned executives can relate several first-hand experiences in which the lawyers involved in a particular issue, especially a labor issue, became absolute rulers at the seat of corporate power. The importance and complexity of the legal implications of a given issue are very real, but the corporate leadership role should not be abdicated when the decisions get tougher. We have never heard of a federal judge or any jury desirous of punishing a company because it openly told the truth. On the contrary, the public record is replete with verdicts awarding millions of dollars to consumers or employees who have been maligned or injured, or have had their lives or reputations damaged, by companies that did not respect the dignity of the individual or the sanctity of the truth.

Congress has provided the Freedom of Information Act to give all citizens and the media equal access to the public record and to curb the authority of government to operate in secrecy. We think the same basic human principle should apply to business. Recognition of the Doctrine of Open Communication as an inviolable right of the individual is a central component of the process of becoming a great company.

The Company with Something Extra

A few companies—ranging in size from small storefront operations to the largest multinational corporations—have been able to nurture and keep alive something special in their business operations. People seem to relate to each other more easily in these companies. The power struggles and politics that are a natural part of organizational life still exist, but the attitude toward them in these companies is healthier, more open. The rules of the game are more widely understood throughout the company. There is an emphasis on *what* is right instead of *who* is right. There is much less secrecy and far more honesty about the realities of business life as they exist for the organization, even if those realities are ambiguous or unpleasant. Employees are expected, as mature adults, to be able to deal with these realities. Sure enough, they do. The tone for this honesty is set at the top of the organization.

Look at Herman Miller, Inc. This middle-sized office furniture manufacturer is headquartered in a small community in western lower Michigan's resort area—Zeeland. It is the premier company in the office furniture systems and products field and has now diversified into health care interiors. The numbers tell but one side of the story. In the face of a harsh recessional economy, for the year ended May 29, 1982, sales reached $314 million, up 24.2 percent, and net income was up 30.5 percent to $18,117,000. Earnings per share were up 21.3 percent; orders were up 25.3 percent, and backlog hit an all-time high of $72,153,000. Not bad for a company which a decade earlier had sales of only $23,453,000 and earnings of $385,000.

Herman Miller had an employee turnover average of only 8 percent for 1980–82, compared with a 25 percent national average. The company's absenteeism is also low: 1.3 percent in 1982 versus the national average of 5.7 percent (and 14 percent for Fridays and Mondays). Herman Miller paid out $1.5 million in extra bonus money to 700 production workers in 1982. But the corporate payoff was much more than the $1 million in cost reduction achieved. Savings were passed on to the consumer and Herman Miller recently cut prices when others in its industry were increasing theirs. This reduced its dealers' costs which in turn increased shipments which, in turn, enabled the company to increase its sales over 50 percent and its earnings 65.5 percent. The momentum has continued. In terms of profitability, Herman Miller's return on stockholder's equity is double that of the contract furniture industry: 16.21 percent versus 8 percent.

A good example of the quality and innovation in communication at Herman Miller is the development of one of the company's newest products, the Ergon chair, introduced four years ago. The design itself was innovative and set a standard that competitors are still seeking to emulate. But what made the introduction of the chair so significant is that the design and marketing plan couldn't have worked without a highly successful internal corporate communication network.

The startling concept was to build chairs for a volume price bracket—more competitive than Herman Miller had previously approached—yet to produce a chair which had typical Herman Miller design and engineering excellence. Market research indicated that other chairs in this price bracket (under $500) were rather undistinguished. It became obvious that a really excellent chair, heavily promoted, had the potential of capturing the market.

The Ergon chair began with *price* as part of its design criteria. A cooperative team effort, typical of Herman Miller's management philosophy, took the rigidity out of all job classifications involved in the Ergon program. The designer was deeply into engineering. The engineering group directly influenced design, and everyone was into marketing. Many hands shared the burden to bring the prototype to final form within budget and on schedule. In one year, the Ergon chair captured its market.

Many factors have contributed to Herman Miller's outstanding success story. For decades the company's leadership, headed by D. J. De Pree and his sons, Max and Hugh, have held a ruthless allegiance to the very best in tasteful design and function and the highest product quality. Max De Pree is fond of saying that Herman Miller has revolutionized the office furniture industry; "not once but twice, and a case could be made for three times—and I don't think we're through." The company has for 30 years effectively used a Scanlon Plan and through this novel profit-and-information-sharing approach has continually shared the fruits of its business operations with all its employees.[1] Equally, it shares with all employees complete information on all aspects of business operations, with that same good taste and attention to quality.

The inherent quality of Herman Miller's communication devices—its newsletters, brochures, and other publications—is equal to that of its fine office furniture. More important, the company has never lost sight of the value of the human touch. Through the Scanlon Plan a series of work-group meetings, both formal and informal, are regularly held each month as a *normal* part of the way the company conducts its business. Employees at Herman

Miller are exceptionally well informed, not only about their own company's operations but also about their chief competitors. In a very real way, the measurable success of Herman Miller can be tied directly to the open, honest, and ongoing dialogue the company strives to maintain with its employees, customers, stockholders—all of its constituents.

What's the payoff in practicing good communication? Bottom-line results for a company whose management is committed to the Doctrine of Open Communication include greater profit, more sustained growth, and the chance to achieve greatness and to assert business leadership on the American scene. Practicing open communication can give your company a competitive edge.

If one examines the growth and success paths of IBM, Xerox, General Foods, General Motors, AT&T, and other leaders of America's major industries, at the core in nearly every case is recognition of the importance of effective communication to the company's business destiny. At a time in American business life when the Japanese are laying down products in the United States at prices and quality levels that are defeating domestic products in the marketplace, and when German and Scandinavian manufacturers are producing automobiles, fountain pens, and an array of finely crafted products that earn respect and a sizable share of the U.S. and other world markets, America's business leaders must relearn the great value of effective communication to business success.

Japanese managers have wisely borrowed the American business principles first enunciated by Elton Mayo, Chester Barnard, Edwards Deming, and Douglas McGregor. Japanese managers have earned their leadership eminence in world business circles because of their consistent and dedicated adherence to applying some of the principles of good people management that first appeared in the literature and factories of U.S. business. That American companies have not more universally embraced these principles is clearly a sorry and costly mistake.

American managers can close the gap. But they have to run at double-time to catch up. How do they go about it?

They must commit themselves to the Doctrine of Open Communication. Secrecy and closed-door policies—long a cherished heritage in many American boardrooms—must be abandoned. We have heard hundreds of times over again the defensive lament "We can't say that; it will help our competition." We have talked with scores of CEOs and senior executives who have insisted, "That's privileged information." Or they have said, regarding their own employees, "It's none of their damned business."

Leadership Power

Robert K. Greenleaf, retired director of management research at AT&T, has written a thoughtful book, *Servant Leadership*, that stands out on the manager's bookshelf among a plethora of models and theories of corporate leadership. In it he describes a potent, compelling bit of wisdom that can't easily be ignored: *the true leader is servant first.*

This proposition appears to be full of contradictions, but this doesn't diminish its truth. The problem isn't that the idea of a servant leader is self-contradictory, but that the idea is dangerous:

> And, as I ponder the fusing of servant and leader, it seems a dangerous creation: dangerous for the natural servant to become a leader, danger- ous for the leader to be a servant first, and dangerous for a follower to insist on being led by a servant. There are safer and easier alternatives available to all three.[2]

The servant-leader idea requires deliberate and imaginative use of leadership power. It calls for some risk. It calls for intelligence and maturity. The simple beauty of the concept will escape many managers. Others will ignore the wisdom it holds, opting for a less risky, more mundane and routine philosophy of leadership. The greatest danger is that while several heads may be nodding, "Yes, that's an intriguing idea," few will have the courage to take a closer look.

Greenleaf tells his story more eloquently than we could. Our purpose is not to elaborate on his notion of the servant leader, but to challenge American executives to think about another impor- tant truth: communication holds the key to the genuine power of leadership in organizations.

All managers have a philosophy of leadership. Douglas McGre- gor taught us that 20 years ago by illustrating how a manager's assumptions about workers, called Theory X and Theory Y, can determine managerial effectiveness. To find out about a manager's leadership philosophy, records can be examined, performance re- viewed, the manager can be interviewed. But the real story is found by listening to the manager's subordinates. Ask any subordinate to tell you about the boss's leadership philosophy and you'll get an honest answer. What's more, the answer will always be informative. Our best leaders actively seek out this kind of feedback from subordinates, knowing that it often requires a thick skin (what one manager we know calls "Epidermal Conditioning") but knowing, too, that one's leadership philosophy is very apparent to subordinates, even though it may be hidden from oneself.

Your leadership philosophy is something that you continually communicate, often quite subtly, to those who work for you. It sets the tone for almost everything that occurs in your organization and is therefore extremely important to your effectiveness as a leader. If you want to know more about it, don't ponder the question yourself. Ask your subordinates. Then be prepared to call on large amounts of courage to listen to what they're saying. Asked in the right way, they will tell you the absolute, undeniable truth. This is precisely the process we try to set in motion for chief executives and senior managers through our Communication Audit.

One of the most important lessons to learn about corporate leadership is that it is not a set of personal traits, not a set of functions or even a pattern of behavior. More than these, leadership is a *relationship.* It's a way of interacting—of communicating—with other individuals according to certain rules adhered to by both leader and followers. Some of these rules are written and catalogued in policy and procedures manuals. Others are the artifacts of culture and social convention. The rules cover such areas as who may initiate interaction, who may terminate interaction, what topics may be discussed, what topics are taboo, and who has access to what information. The rules are greatly influenced by the leadership philosophy, set by the people at the top, that permeates the organization.

When subordinates share their knowledge about the boss's leadership philosophy, they provide insight into the use of power in the organization. What is power?

May the Force Be with You

Sociologists have categorized power according to the methods used to exercise it, assigning it such adjectives as "coercive," "normative," "legitimate," and "remunerative." The differences among these categories are boring and relatively unimportant to our topic. In all cases, power inevitably has to do with influence over other people. In organizational terms, we mean "power" to signify not only the authority connected with one's status, position, or credentials but also—and this is most significant—the human energy quickly sensed by others that tells them "this person has integrity." This quality is elusive. It is more emotional and spiritual than physical. Both men and women can have it. Charisma is not quite it, for it is much less showy. Nor is it the same, in the language of "Star Wars," as the Force that enables Luke Skywalker to prevail over the evil Darth Vader. Business leadership's source of this power is much less mysterious.

A number of successful companies and their chief executives provide case studies of this leadership power in action. One unassuming example is Diet Center. Less than 10 years old, the company has grown dramatically from Sybil Ferguson's good ideas on how to lose weight, which worked for her and then for a few friends. It has now blossomed into an international corporation that gains 56,000 customers every six weeks. Mrs. Ferguson and her husband Roger and son Michael have provided the leadership that built for them a company that grosses more than $90 million a year. The company is entirely self-sufficient, not relying on any outside suppliers in delivering its service. A new Diet Center opens somewhere every day. In the Franchise 500, the annual listing compiled by *Entrepreneur* magazine, Diet Center was rated number 9 in 1981 and number 6 in 1982, ahead of such names as Burger King, McDonald's, Midas Muffler, and Kentucky Fried Chicken. All this from the little rural community of Rexburg, Idaho, population 11,000, where Diet Center's headquarters have grown from 22 employees in 1978 to over 285 today. How did they do it?

> A keystone of the foundation on which this company is built is sincerity and genuine interest in the people they serve, the people who make up the corporate staff. *It may sound somewhat corny, but this wholesome, joyful approach to doing business has created one of the most effective business operations in America today.*[3] (Emphasis added.)

Of course, there is nothing corny about it at all. Have we become so afraid of showing genuine interest in people in corporate America? Have we become so jaded that we consider sincerity corny? What the Fergusons have achieved, after all, is a marvelous demonstration of leadership *power*.

We asked Jim Liljenquist, Sybil Ferguson's assistant, who has been with the company since 1978, to describe what it's like to work for Diet Center:

It's a wonderful experience. Roger and Sybil are still very actively involved on an everyday basis and in every aspect of this business. Their style is to communicate directly with the people who are actually doing the job and to draw from their first-hand experience, in addition to relying upon the traditional brain trust at the head of the corporation. People here feel a part of the cause to which we are all dedicated— helping overweight people overcome their problem . . . and this is seen as much more than a job.

There is a high level of trust and honesty throughout the Diet Center organization. For instance, we have been approached several times by direct-mail organizations who were willing to pay premium prices to obtain a mailing list of Diet Center patrons. Sybil has never consented to sell these lists because it would represent a violation of that trust. Similarly, open communication is practiced with the franchisees in the field; all corporate matters are aired with the entire organization in advance of a decision. Everyone works together toward a common goal, and, I might add, they work harder knowing that they are part of the team.[4]

The Fergusons seem to practice effective communication instinctively. Some corporate leaders learn about the power of human communication late in their careers. Having matured and grown personally over the years, they finally begin to adjust and adapt their own behavior in light of what they have learned, albeit late in the game. Too many managers just pay lip service to communication, often quite convincingly, without ever changing themselves or without genuinely understanding what it means to listen with sensitivity or to speak the simple truth. It is rare for a manager to demonstrate through his or her behavior a keen awareness that the process of communication is so much more than just writing and speaking.

Information and communication are different. Western business culture has placed an overemphasis on the role and value of information in management. Classic business school education allocates a disproportionate share of the curriculum to the technical analysis of information in the decision-making process. Almost no time is spent in recognition of the principle that every decision has to be communicated and *the way it is communicated* greatly determines how it is accepted and carried out or whether it is accepted at all.

Information is inanimate, logical, objective. Communication is a process; it is subjective, perceptual, and continual. The rules that govern the analysis of information and its storage and retrieval do not apply to communication. Business operations can be examined by applying analytic techniques to quantitative information. The analysis of communication relies on qualitative judgment, perceptions of others, intuition, and human sensitivity.

Leadership power involves both information and communication. American business has paid too much attention to the technical use of information and has ignored the real potential of communication. When push comes to shove, the latter is vastly more important to corporate leadership. So say four of the leading scholars and practitioners in the field of corporate information systems in their recent book, *Information Strategies: New Pathways to Corporate Power*—Gerald M. Goldhaber, Harry S. Dennis, Gary M. Richetto, and Osmo A. Wiio.

> More often than not, failure at the highest of organizational levels results from the lack of interpersonal (as opposed to technical) competencies. Even in technically based industries or government agencies, engineering or scientific skills become secondary to interpersonal, behavioral, communication skills as one ascends the hierarchy.[5]

Similar words have been said by countless numbers of enlightened managers and management consultants over the years. Communication skill is the essence of effective corporate leadership, and it becomes increasingly essential as people move up the corporate ladder or into positions of broad public responsibility in government, the professions, and, increasingly, technology and the sciences.

Volumes have been written about leadership. Psychologists, sociologists, and behaviorists have been and for generations in the future will be dissecting powerful leaders in all walks of life to determine how they got that way. It is fascinating to study how the individual wielder of power intertwines and uses communication, the power of personality, and other intangible traits in a rare combination so precious that the tide of history has been turned.

In the corporate setting powerful leaders abound. Harold Geneen at International Telephone and Telegraph Corporation had great abilities as organizer and manager of that international conglomerate. His monthly meetings with hundreds of managers flown in from the farthest reaches of the ITT empire were masterful building blocks of organizational effectiveness. They were also instruments of communication but in a very special sense were limited to the transmission of planning and programming information from chief manager to subordinate managers.

Those close to Geneen probably would not give him good grades for the use of communication in interpersonal relationships. He did not himself have a great deal of the persuasive and congenial force of personality that combine into an essential ingredient of wisely using communication techniques as instruments of leadership power by the intelligent executive, yet he was an effective executive and during his tenure at ITT achieved growth and profits that set new records. His style of leadership was to entrust broad grants of power in the communication area to his corporate staff officer, Edward J. Gerrity, Jr., senior vice president and director of corporate relations and advertising. Gerrity knew his boss well, and the two made a polished team. Their symbiotic relationship bears out our thesis that the communicator and the CEO boss must fly in tight formation. They must be made of similar stuff intellectually and in character, and their personalities must be closely compatible.

On the other hand, as you examine the personal grace of Thomas J. Watson, Jr., during those years when he ran International Business Machines Corporation, you find a different type of leader at work. Watson had a deep commitment to the power and practical day-to-day use of good public relations techniques. We doubt that he thought of himself as a public relations practitioner. In every way, however, he was indeed the most effective single interpreter and symbol of IBM as a great corporation.

If we did a thorough and scientific analysis of Watson as leader and as communicator, we think we could demonstrate a highly successful and sharply defined doctrine of leadership at the top. IBM's most popular CEO used practices that accorded respect to the individual while at the same time nurturing growth in a super-high-technology corporation. This process has made possible the organizing of thousands of employees into the mighty corporation which today is respected everywhere, is highly profitable, and is the undisputed leader in the computer industry. All in the industry watch what "Big Blue" is doing. Would that they all communicated as well as IBM.

Let's turn for a moment to the world of higher education. American colleges and universities have become major organizational entities not unlike corporations. When you examine education for leaders who were good communicators, one of the names that stands preeminent is Robert Maynard Hutchins. Hutchins became Dean of the Yale University Law School at age 27. Trustees of the University of Chicago identified him as a star in 1929, and at 29 he became the youngest president of a major university in the history of American education. His personal presence, his keen intellect, his wit, and his sensitivity as a human being were inspiring. He moved faculty, students, trustees, business executives, and community leaders to higher levels of excellence.

Hutchins reorganized the curriculum at the University of Chicago to put major emphasis on the humanities. He initiated Chicago's policy of admitting bright teenagers early to the university. His communication skill, coupled with his intellect and his recognition of the need to bring educational advancement to the general population, led to the creation of the Great Books program. Having a marvelous sense of the important role business could play in education, he built close ties to the business community in Chicago.

Never were Hutchins' communication and leadership skills more adroitly demonstrated than in 1949 when he was cochairman of the Goethe Bicentennial Foundation. The foundation sponsored a month-long world scholars' convocation and music festival in Aspen, Colorado, as the focal point for the American observance of Goethe's greatness as statesman, poet, educator, playwright, philosopher, and scientist.

One of us had the privilege of working closely with Hutchins that year by virtue of responsibility for handling all of the foundation's communications for the convocation and music festival. Walter P. Paepcke, the CEO of Container Corporation of America, the foundation's other cochair, and Hutchins were seeking a single world figure to personify Goethe's concept of Universal Man.

It was Hutchins who found just the right solution: bring Albert Schweitzer to Aspen from his jungle hospital in Lambarene, French Equatorial Africa. More than anyone, Schweitzer embodied the spirit of Universal Man in his life's work. Dr. Schweitzer was a famed medical missionary, the world's foremost exponent of Bach on the organ, a biographer of Bach, a professor at the University of Strasbourg, a physician and surgeon, and a humanist whose compassion matched that of Goethe. Schweitzer, who was later to receive the Nobel Peace Prize, was the perfect symbol for an educational-communications event that has probably not been equaled since.

The world leaders in literature, art, music, and scholarship who converged on Aspen in June and July over 30 years ago later gave birth to the Aspen Institute for Humanistic Studies. These events demonstrate the close working partnership that is possible between America's great business leaders and the luminaries of the educational world. It is such a revived partnership that is now so urgently needed to energize the leadership for the renaissance in communication.[6]

All these great leaders have common threads of humanity which come together in an ability to weave spiritual, inspirational, and even political ambitions into a life plan of service and fellowship to other human beings. This is really what Robert K. Greenleaf is talking about in *Servant Leadership.*

The qualities of these respecters of the dignity of the individual and servants of the community are often found in the makeup of the general managers and the owner-operators of small businesses throughout the nation. We think the real heroes of our business society are not necessarily the executives who may earn a million dollars per year in lucrative contracts replete with heavy stock options and lush perks, but often rather the president of a small short-line farm equipment company in Nebraska, or the general manager of a mid-sized industrial equipment manufacturing company in Minnesota, or the nun who is the chief administrator at a Catholic hospital in Omaha. All are daily demonstrating the great power of leadership through human communication.

We want tomorrow's generation of business leaders to study closely and learn from these dimensions of true leadership, expressed through caring and thoughtful human interpersonal communication.

You Can Feel the Chemistry

In great companies whose managers practice open communication as an inherent part of good business leadership, you can feel the chemistry and see its evidence at work in every facet of daily business operations. You can sense it when you walk in the door. In such companies the employees have a legitimate sense of their importance, genuine pride in their work, respect (even admiration) for the men and women at the top. From the top, managers running things have an instinctive warmth, cordiality, and sense of authentic interest in the lives and welfare of fellow employees.

Is this a fairy tale? Do such environments actually exist in corporate America?

Anyone who doubts that such a climate of mutual respect and openness really can exist has not opened his or her eyes and ears to the difference between thousands of run-of-the-mill, mediocre businesses and the small number of truly great ones. These excep-

tions do not exist only on the pages of the *Wall Street Journal,*
Forbes, or *Fortune.* They can be found throughout the quiet regions
of sometimes scruffy, backyard America. Let us describe one such
gem of a company: Kansas Farm Bureau in Manhattan, Kansas.

This is a 75-year-old farm cooperative with its own special character and stamp of excellence. It is a $250 million–asset operation
with seven profit centers, each a strong and growing business. There
are life insurance companies, casualty companies, financial services,
and merchandising and retailing operations. All operate under a
consolidated senior management group.

In bottom-line terms, this assemblage of seven corporations earns
a consistent and steadily increasing 5 to 7 percent net on revenue.
The executive vice president and chief operating officer is John R.
Graham, a trim 36-year-old graduate of the University of Arkansas.
We asked Graham how much of his time is spent on the task of
communicating:

> The whole business day. Now that's using communication in the broad-
> est sense. It may be communication in the form of being seen in a
> work area where special projects are going on, just to let them know
> that you support them, and maybe patting a couple of the appropriate
> people on the back or giving them a little push at the right time.[7]

Why should executives and managers change their present systems of communication, spend the additional sums of money and
invest the time and executive effort to achieve the substantially
higher levels of excellence in communication that we counsel? Because it is worth it. It is good business. If the process is conscientiously followed, the growth of your business enterprise will be
healthier and you will tap the most valuable asset in the entire
business world—the latent talents, abilities, and ideas of your employees.

Does this smack of manipulation? Is it using people? Of course
not. It is important to not confuse an open environment with one
that requires compliance to arbitrary dictates through coercion, subtle manipulation, or autocratic repression. Given the chance, your
employees will jump at the opportunity to give more of themselves—
their creativity, brain power, innovative ideas, thoughtful analysis,
considered opinions—as long as they believe the opportunity to
do so is genuinely and sincerely provided.

We believe that at least 25 percent of the human potential in
the typical American corporation today lies untapped and wasted.
This is not because people are lazy, undermanaged, or unwilling

to work. It is largely because they have not been provided the genuine opportunity to give their full measure. In many instances, they have been so completely turned off by an uncaring management that they give only the minimum. They yearn to give more, but they have lost trust.

Measuring the Turn-On

If by some magical power it was possible to apply all of these principles of good communication to business and industry throughout the United States, the 25 percent added output could legitimately increase the GNP $750 billion, could earn an additional $45 billion in net profits for the industrial superstructure of America, and would release a flow of creativity and spawn a new generation of inventiveness never before seen in the history of modern business. If a 25 percent potential for improvement is reasonable, think what could happen if we were able to massage this a little more and reach 35 percent or 50 percent.

Recognizing the skeptics and the frustrations of past experiences with similar efforts to achieve improvements in productivity, we submit that we are not talking about industrial engineering improvements, work simplification, redesign of equipment, or the use of any of the standard systems currently being universally applied in business and industry. Our premise and the basis of this book are that the human potential in the American worker is not now fully or well utilized. In Japanese offices and factories, managers have been more successful in applying many of these originally American concepts we advocate by using the peculiar and distinctive framework of Japanese culture, Japan's managerial system, and the heritage of the work ethic unique to that island nation. The American work ethic and the heritage of the U.S. worker are just as rich, and they have greater potential than anywhere in the world. Our argument is that the nation is sadly served today because the present generation of business managers is not tapping the hidden creative potential of the American workforce.

We need to reharness the strength in the American workforce and tap into the rich heritage interwoven in the business enterprises that make up the fabric of our nation. If we do reenergize this mighty Yankee industrial machine of ours, the rewards will well satisfy any board of directors, group of stockholders, or hard-nosed CEO.

CHAPTER 10

Making the Renaissance Happen

A teacher who can arouse a feeling for one single good action, for one single good poem, accomplishes more than he who fills our memory with rows on rows of natural objects, classified with name and form.

Johann Wolfang von Goethe

NOT ALL CORPORATE LEADERS in American companies are ready and able to make the commitment to open communication. There are certain managers whose personal styles, combined with a management environment firmly entrenched in secrecy and close-fisted behavior, effectively block the expression of sensitive and caring behavior. Part of the price these business leaders must pay if they want to adopt the Doctrine of Open Communication is the psychic pain inherent in changing their personal behavior and management style. There are no short cuts to such change.

Top-Down Commitment

The business executives we visualize as moving into action to apply our thesis are those who know the importance of good communication and are anxious to apply these ideas but need access to new research and new thinking about how to initiate the change process. This is going to take solid determination to override the standard objections we have heard for nearly a decade: "We are already doing this"; "We just did a communications survey"; "We have been analyzing employee attitudes for the past five years."

Industry's typical piecemeal approach to getting a handle on the effectiveness of corporate communication through a survey of employee attitudes, or a series of surveys, invariably results in a row of chronologically arranged notebooks that serve little purpose and merely accumulate dust on the bookshelves of vice presidents for human resources. Surveys can be useful instruments in providing documentation of the change process. But they are only a small part—the easiest part—of the important process of analyzing where a company might start to improve internal and external communication effectiveness. They do not *produce* change.

For effective change, companies and their top leaders should be open and willing to support programs that evolve from underwriting research and development in communication akin to the level of R & D commitments for new products and services. While examining opportunities for fresh ideas and applying funding for R & D in communication as an instrument of corporate leadership, management should be open to applying such seemingly inappropriate concepts as art therapy, music, and poetry and drama as additional forms of organizational communication.

Branching Out

Nurturing the human spirit is a dimension of our work life that should not be foreign to American business and industry. Corporate sponsorship of great dramas on television and funding for the arts have now become an accepted mode of business behavior for scores of companies. Public television is enriched, the public enjoys the arts, and business makes honest gains in being better understood through such commitments to artistic excellence and cultural programming.

Why not take the next logical step? Use the creative arts as another dimension of corporate communication. Many of the newer creative therapies use the arts as a form of healing. Art therapy uses painting, drawings, sculpture, and even textiles as forms of personal communication to express and relieve emotion. Horticultural therapy does the same with indoor and outdoor gardening. Poetry, drama, and dance and motion therapy all are effectively employed to transmit messages full of human expression. Some people find it hard to express in words feelings that are more easily given meaning in movement, color, or poetic cadence. Who is to say this is any less legitimate and effective than the spoken or written word? Why not expand the boundaries of the human spirit, give flight to feeling, and convey human expression using *all* the multidimensional levels of emotional transference of meaning?

What Deere & Company achieved through its sponsorship of the John Deere Artist in Residence program was a pioneering form of in-plant corporate communication. Pianist Barbara Nissman performed at community concerts under Deere sponsorship. She spent time working with gifted children in the local community and even hosted her own television program on public TV. These facets of the program added up to a clear positive message about the company, communicated to all of its many audiences, both internal and external.

To employees the message was "We respect you as individuals. We want you to produce quality farm equipment to high standards. Only fine workers operating to high levels of excellence can accomplish these goals. Similar goals motivate concert artists. Great composers were moved by wellsprings of human greatness and enriched our lives. We can all benefit when we strive toward this high standard—and the community is rewarded too." It was yet another way to express good business citizenship.

Little theater groups in communities for years have been using the stage for constructive and rewarding community endeavor. Why not use theater arts as a form of communication for some forms of corporate messages which lend themselves to this creative form of expression? Go the next mile, and transfer drama to the work setting as yet another form of communication. In a generation of computers talking to computers and electronic signals bouncing in from satellites, why not bring people together by enabling human communication to rise to its fullest level of creative expression using all the communication arts?

Anthony J. F. O'Reilly, president and CEO of H. J. Heinz Company, has already committed the 1982 Heinz annual report to this imaginative use of the arts. A worldwide poetry contest for employees generated 700 entries from 300 Heinz people, from secretaries to forklift operators to a plant superintendent. Winners were selected by two noted professors of English, were published in full pages in the annual report, and were illustrated by full-page paintings commissioned from leading artists. O'Reilly feels this is a new way to communicate "the character of those who work for Heinz."

Employees would find this form of participative management challenging and, initially, a bit curious. This too can be an effective form of team building that we believe will bring benefits to the bottom line. Yes, we realize that some managers will be flabbergasted because this idea hasn't yet become chapter and verse in the personnel handbooks. But what is pioneering all about if not the creative transfer of a successful concept to a new application—and a little risk taking?

Will it pay off? Is it worth the cost in extra dollars and extra effort? Can we afford it?

Money is the least expensive part of this equation.

What does the best in communication cost? In many companies management is already paying the price but ironically is not receiving the benefit that the budget expenditure should provide. Such hapless companies often have large departments for corporate communication—some prefer the more "in" name "public affairs"— but by whatever title the communication function is known, our experience suggests that as much as half of its true mission is being missed. When you apply that to the more than $30 billion we estimate were spent in 1982 for all forms of corporate communication— internal and external—by the U.S. business and industrial establishment worldwide, you must face up to a gigantic waste of money. But more significant, precious human resources are being squandered that our economy and nation can ill afford.

In most instances, it is unnecessary to throw even one more dollar into this multi-billion-dollar debacle. Our experience has led us to the conclusion that the present dollar resources currently committed are probably more than sufficient, but they're misplaced and carelessly allocated.

Second Best Won't Do

Our advice to chief executive officers in any business is to never settle for anything less than the best in communication. Don't put in position second-rate managers as professional communicators. Find the bright stars and give them room to grow and to be creative. And then back them up and follow their judgment and instincts within the framework of their professional expertise. Insist that they be broad-gauge people who are not only skillful communicators, sensitive to the human relations side of business, but also competent in marketing. Insist that they be able to read a balance sheet and be effective in interpersonal communication with the chief financial officer and other managers. Make sure they know the importance of the security analyst and are able to maintain the mutually respectful rapport that the public company must cultivate with the professional investment community as well as its shareholder constituency. They also must be adept in community and government relations, be possessed of an ability to understand the technical and engineering side of business, and understand how to use opinion and attitude research in its many forms.

Do not let your industrial relations department stand in opposition to your communications department. In too many companies, the industrial relations types are in command of communication, and the result is a sorry diluted mixture of legalism and narrow-range thinking that inhibits the free flow of good ideas and the cultivation of the atmosphere of openness and trust that is the *sine qua non* of the great company.

Communications officers are most effective when they report directly to the CEO. These key corporate players are an extension of the boss's office. They are the strategists, the skilled craftsmen and the expert counselors who enrich and enliven the CEO's personal commitment and devotion to good communication. The CEO and the communication officer should function as a duality. They are best when they have compatible chemistry. In the ideal situation, the communication officer knows how the boss is thinking and can take the kernel of an idea and carry it forward. The communication officer should be the CEO's alter ego in communications planning. When this type of rapport and trust is soundly structured and operating smoothly, no one can easily tell where the CEO's own language and thought leave off and his communication officer's input takes over. The professional communication officer should be a valued ally and a vital part of overall top corporate strategy.

Operating in this mode costs money. Don't skimp on the budgetary commitment to good communication. In all respects, go first class. That is the soundest and truest way to reap first-class benefits and results that will pay for the program many times over through a workforce enjoying high job satisfaction, quality work output, and a steeper profit curve. Beyond the financial cost, the CEO ought to be willing to learn and, often, to accept the need to change his or her own behavior.

Who Teaches the Leader?

In many cases, seasoned and successful CEOs are going to have to undergo special training in communications. We have long been conscious of the difficulty faced by the chairman or president who, upon reaching the top of the ladder, finds he or she must cope with a serious problem: where does the leader go to learn how to be a better leader?

We know of no resource currently available to senior officers that will teach this elite group the lessons and techniques they may have never learned in their climb to the top about how to use effective communication principles in the day-to-day execution of their responsibilities. Rank makes it awkward to learn from one's subordinates, though we naturally recognize that subordinates can sometimes be excellent teachers. Some insights can be gleaned by interaction with other top executives and through the resources of the Conference Board, Business Roundtable, Committee for Economic Development, or Harvard's summer program for executives. All of these are helpful services, but we see entirely new training resources having to be created.

We suggest that the more enlightened of the graduate business schools can team up with industry to forge a new partnership dedicated to mounting individualized and practical programs that can address some of these top executive learning needs.

Other senior executives, particularly where proprietary information is involved or the degree of confidentiality is high, are better off using consultants to custom-design company-sponsored seminars and senior-officer skill development workshops in communication techniques and strategy.

We have used an innovative Communication Workshop concept for certain of our clients where we have intermixed the board of directors, all senior operating management, divisional officers, and veteran plant foremen in a seminar with splendid results. By getting these vastly different levels of the corporate hierarchy to talk to one another without barriers and pulling no punches, insights are cultivated about the power of communication and the change process that can have profound effects at all levels in companies.

Imagine, if you will, a U-shaped grouping of tables with all senior officers, a half-dozen outside directors, and the major divisional heads of a $55 million company all assembled in one room. They are listening to a panel of a half-dozen experienced foremen unload their ideas. We did such a training exercise in the summer of 1981 in Kansas City with noteworthy results. Directors, in particular, were astounded at the knowledge and sound economic understanding these factory floor veterans possessed. Their sensitivity to waste, their understanding of human nature, and their know-how about where and how to save time and money were eye-opening. That type of session is beyond the scope of a business school. But underwritten by the company and run by seasoned consultants, such training holds great promise. However, senior officers must be willing to put a lot of themselves into such sessions. They must be tough-minded and thick-skinned enough to signal that authentic freedom of expression is encouraged. In this atmosphere, the CEO and the people at the top are going to learn a lot. From that experience, they can secure their guerrilla skills in communication and produce results that can be measured in increased profit opportunities and larger market shares.

Communication as Profit Center

For almost three decades we have heard it said that good communication is a *cost* of doing business. In the conventional mode and reflecting the ways the educational system produces men and women who struggle to communicate adequately, some feel that communication is an overhead expense. But it need not be. If it is properly organized and structured as a working part of business strategy and day-to-day leadership at the top, we believe the communication function can be utilized as an activity that can pay its own way. Because communication can have a direct and measurable influence on profitability, it should be structured and treated as a profit center. Other divisional and departmental managers need to be trained and encouraged by senior management to call upon and use the communication professionals in the company as valued corporate resources. When communication is organized in this manner and supported by a strong mandate from the top, with the communications officer freed from constantly wasting time and effort selling his or her mission to others, concentration can be applied to creating programs that are soundly tied to strategic planning and are executed with imagination and quality.

In a company practical enough to apply the principle of a profit center to good business communication, the other staff department heads and the varied operational divisions of the business enterprise will learn to seek out the communication specialists to aid them in their respective areas of responsibility. Sales will come easier based on better customer understanding of what the company and its product lines stand for in the way of product integrity. The significance of the company's research, development, and engineering programs will be more clearly understood by the marketplace. Operating in this manner and supported by positive communication behavior at the top, engineering and technical specialists within the company will gradually join forces with the creative minds in the communication department to help forge a true team effort. Such a multidisciplinary business approach will always be more successful because the players will be better able not only to articulate their own ideas and thoughts but also to cultivate the support and understanding of people with ancillary work functions. This across-the-board cooperation can be cultivated and strengthened by each understanding the other's job more fully—a condition which is best attained in companies practicing open communication.

Business planners and the corporate development experts should talk early on with the corporate communications specialists about strategy and long-range implementation of programs. Good communication professionals need ample lead times to coordinate and organize the often complex channels for corporate communication needed to reach multiple and diverse audiences. When all segments of the enterprise are trained and comfortable in this mutually respectful cooperation, then the ability to position the company on the cutting edge of new markets, new technologies, and broadened international opportunities for growth and profit will come easier and faster.

This is the way to prepare for the future in your business and industry. These concepts work equally well applied to small businesses, in education, in the not-for-profit sector, in government, and in health services. If the lessons of history and past performance are programmed to aid the future, the challenges of growth and sustained profitability will be more easily achieved, made possible by a communication mandate well executed and supported by a commitment from the leaders at the top. If all know that the total business is dedicated to the principle that they all know where they are going and have a well-designed roadmap to accomplish the objectives set for tomorrow, then wheels at all levels will turn with precision. The price is not in money alone. The price is paid in personal dedication, going the extra distance to demonstrate respect for the individual and support for the human spirit. Fresh ideas, innovative thinking, sensitivity to the feelings of employees, customers, stockholders, suppliers, and other business associates—all abound in the progressive company whose CEO and top leaders daily practice good communication.

For the company whose management takes these commitments to heart, the final cost is small compared with the potential gains. Adapting to this mode of business behavior and universal respect for the dignity of the individual is the most direct and effective way of beating Japanese management at the game of producing fine-quality products in world markets at competitive prices. And such conduct will yield a more humane form of industrial society as American management faces the year 2000.

American industry cannot afford to do less. Here is how David K. Easlick, president of Michigan Bell, characterizes the price he was willing to pay for good communication and all of its resulting benefits:

> I had the persistent feeling that, somehow, we could be more effective if we were more open with each other—if we trusted each other more—if we could better communicate with each other. . . . It became depressingly obvious that the major problem was *me*, the way *I* was managing: *my* management style! Inside, I remember being angry, hurt, and faintly sick.[1]

The startling enlightenment that Mr. Easlick describes is the personal basis of a genuine renaissance in American corporate leadership. It is achieved through the conscious recognition of the power that lies dormant in the human mind and spirit and the untapped human resources already at work in America.

Making It Work

In the previous chapter, we described Herman Miller, Inc., as a prime example of an American company with something extra—with the ability to put into practice the Doctrine of Open Communication and make it work. To learn first-hand how Herman Miller's chief executive officer uses communication as an instrument of managerial leadership and to examine how the whole concept works, day in and day out, we spent a day with Max De Pree, chairman.

Max's father, D. J. De Pree, founded the company, and at 91

still comes to the office and has an active interest in the business, though leadership at the top has since passed to Max. Hugh De Pree, Max's brother, has also played a very key role at Herman Miller, serving as CEO for seventeen years before Max assumed the responsibilities as CEO and chairman.

Max De Pree is in his late fifties, white-haired, courtly, and easy to talk to. He has a philosophic bent, reads widely, cares about people, and is respected and liked by the company's workforce. His style has fostered an easygoing cordiality in the personal relationships between management and workers. There is not much standing on traditional corporate ceremony. First names are routinely used, and the CEO is "Max" to factory workers and office staff alike.

All work areas in the plants are exposed to windows. Work bays look out upon landscaped courtyards where outdoor furniture makes open-air work breaks inviting. Fresh cut flowers and blooming plants adorn rest areas, and convenient informational kiosks give workers easy access to timely information about the business. Well-organized, clean, and color-coded bulletin boards post up-to-the-minute information for all to see.

The business is run on the basis of a mutually respectful worker/ management relationship that is a model for American industry. It didn't get that way overnight. Years of hard work, experimentation, and open-mindedness made it happen. And the workforce, 3,500 employees, has responded handsomely to the leadership example set at the top.

Let's let Max De Pree tell his own story in his own words:

> I think that leadership probably has more to do with the quality side of the business than the quantity side. Leadership has more to do with the values and principles and standards than it does with the consequences of those values, principles, and standards. I believe that leadership is also much more strategic than management. One way to look at leadership is to say that the first responsibility of leadership is to define reality. The last responsibility is to say "thank you." And there is a heck of a lot in between, of course. To say "thank you" is one of the least understood but most effective ways to behave.
>
> Three of the key elements in the art of working together are how to deal with change, how to deal with conflict, and how to reach our potential. A legal contract almost always breaks down under the duress of conflict and change. This is the point where the need for what I have called covenantal relationships can be seen so clearly.

A covenantal relationship is one which is based on shared commitment to ideas, to issues, to values, to goals, and to management processes. Words such as "love," "warmth," "personal chemistry" are certainly pertinent. Covenantal relationships are open to influence. They fill deep needs, and they enable work to have meaning and to be fulfilling. Covenantal relationships reflect unity and grace and poise. They are an expression of the sacred nature of relationships. Covenantal relationships enable corporations to be hospitable to the unusual person and to unusual ideas. Covenantal relationships tolerate risk and forgive errors. I'm convinced that the best management process for today's environment is participative management based on covenantal relationships.

What I'm talking about is the perfectly rational business of moving to a new level of competence in a new and changing era. The way to do this is to understand who we are and to build on the competence that we've developed to date. To seek some insight into the future. To set our goals. To set them high. This, I believe, is both the *privilege* and the *responsibility* of leadership. Effective leadership involves demonstrating a recognition of the rights of the individual. I suggest the following list of person's rights with the idea that this is what leadership owes to those they wish to lead. This is not a complete list, but I believe these eight are essential.

1. THE RIGHT TO BE NEEDED. Are you, as my manager, going to provide me with a genuine opportunity to use my gifts?

2. THE RIGHT TO BE INVOLVED. We need to take action— how are we together going to translate our interaction into products and services on behalf of our users?

3. THE RIGHT TO A COVENANTAL RELATIONSHIP. This is one which is based on shared commitments to ideas, to issues, to values, to goals, and to processes.

4. THE RIGHT TO UNDERSTAND. We all need to know our mission and the direction of our group, our personal career path, what my opportunities are, and how I can realize them. We need to know how tough the competition is. We need to understand and be at home in our human and physical environments. Business leadership must communicate, to educate, to evaluate, to provide understanding.

5. THE RIGHT TO AFFECT ONE'S OWN DESTINY. Few elements in the work process are as important to personal dignity as the opportunity to influence one's own future.

6. THE RIGHT TO BE ACCOUNTABLE. We need to have an opportunity to make a contribution to the group's goals and to share in the ownership of the group's problems.

7. THE RIGHT TO MAKE A COMMITMENT. One of the key responsibilities of leadership is the obligation to be rational.
8. THE RIGHT TO APPEAL. We need to build into our group structures a nonthreatening avenue of appeal.

Work is one of our greatest privileges, and I believe that work should be and can be:

productive and rewarding,
meaningful and maturing,
enriching and fulfilling,
demanding and challenging,
healing and joyful.

It is fundamental to this idea that the needs of the group are best met when, in the process, we meet the needs of the individual persons. An effective organization should be a place of realized potential, both corporate and personal. I am proposing the idea that by lifting our sights and reaching for this vision, we cannot only solve our problems of effectiveness and productivity, but that we may at the same time fundamentally alter the concept of work.

My goal for Herman Miller is that when people both inside the company and outside the company look at all of us, not as a corporation but as a group of people working within a covenantal relationship, they'll say, "Those folks are a gift to the spirit."[2]

Is it any wonder that Max De Pree and Herman Miller and its people are so successful?

Bank of America's Way

How does a new leader at the top go about stimulating the communication openness that is so vital to profitability and future growth? Samuel H. Armacost, the 43-year-old new president and chief executive officer at BankAmerica Corporation in San Francisco, is deeply into that task. We selected BankAmerica as a worthy company to examine closely because its success story is well known, its origins springing from the innovative leadership of founder A. P. Giannini.

In the banking industry and in the communications profession, BankAmerica has long been known for its sound communications. When Louis B. Lundborg was chairman, he became the extroverted and likable spokesman for the bank. He helped humanize the bank's image. John J. Bell, senior vice president, joined BankAmerica in June 1977 and in five years revitalized its communications program.

Business Week in its 1979 cover story on "The Company Image" called Bell one of the top 10 names in corporate public relations. He died in the early fall of '82 but has left a legacy of fine communication that is now being expanded, shifted, and reanalyzed by Armacost to keep pace with the massive changes altering the strategy and game plan for banking and traditional financial services.

The world's largest bank, BankAmerica has 86,000 employees working in more than 2,000 offices in 101 countries. It has 4.2 million customers and 10 to 11 million accounts in the California market, which account for some 35 percent of all banking transactions in the nation's most populous state. Its assets of $121 billion exceed second-ranked Citicorp's $119 billion. BankAmerica assets are nearly twice those of Prudential Insurance, or the combined assets of Sears, Roebuck, Merrill Lynch, and Shearson/American Express.

To get the personal story of how Samuel Armacost is tackling his task of reshaping the strategy and the business destiny of this behemoth, we talked with Armacost. He was remarkably candid and open, a hallmark of his management style. We asked Armacost what communication channels he uses to get his messages through to his workforce.

> Well, I guess we use every device known to man at this moment. We have magazines, both domestic and foreign. One is oriented to articles stressing ways to improve management and we try and place skill-related messages there. Others are informational in terms of what is happening in and around the institution.
>
> We put other messages on video in an effort to appeal to those people who by inclination or by habit in our culture are more television-oriented. Weekly bulletins are used to transmit information and news about changes of an organizational or management nature or market-oriented.
>
> Oftentimes I have found it helps to use outside media interviews as a way to send messages to the internal audience. National magazines are closely read and followed by our people, and I have found that when I send them information as a part of a national publication, it tends to have more credibility even though they may have heard the same message internally six times over. It's amazing. People will accept as gospel what they see on TV or read in the newspapers. But, often, the rest of the information we send them internally simply slides by without apparent notice.
>
> I accept this third-party credibility as a given fact, and we try and use the external media as part of our overall communication strat-

egy. There is a risk in using this tactic, but we have felt pretty good about the messages that were captured this way. Thus we try to be open and available to the external media as opposed to being close-mouthed for fear we will be misquoted.

Our banking industry poses special problems for us. The pace of change in our industry is being set by forces over which we have little control. We have responded to change constantly and are faced with the task of explaining and interpreting change to our people. Our industry is affected by competition which is not regulated, and yet we can respond strategically only to the extent that we are given leeway in Congress and elsewhere. We've tried to make the messages to our staff address these realities of regulation and the competitive marketplace.

We have spent a lot of time talking to our people about this present change process in our business, and we have talked about the impact Merrill Lynch and Sears, Roebuck will be making. Two years ago when I chaired our California Division's management conference, I picked that as my theme. But I would suspect that the audience didn't accept 30 percent of my message that they would soon be worrying about Sears and Merrill Lynch. But we told them that would be the case. Today, there are almost no nonbelievers out there.

In tackling this task of interpreting change to our employees, we are using every conceivable form of communication—print, video, meetings, oral communication, bulletins, and position papers—and we are constantly evaluating the success of the various methods.

Sitting where I do, I have found that one makes some assumptions about communication that generally are invalid. The filters to good communication in the institution are much greater than I thought. In an effort to override those filters, I have relied more heavily on group meetings. My messages get through fairly well in small groups because there is a chance for interaction and the opportunity to clarify side issues and to talk more personally with our people.

It is much harder to send those same messages to your whole population in print because if you are in a strategy formulation area, for example, you cannot control the interpretation of them. It is harder in print to convey any kind of personality. That's why we are probably going to use the video medium a little more and orchestrate more messages from senior officers addressing groups of employees than we have in the past.

In all of our communications to our employees, we try and encourage a feedback process. We stress to them that we care, we ask them to tell us what they think, and we always emphasize that we will give them an honest answer. If we don't know the answer, we tell them we'll get you one.

We are trying to stress in our communications to our employees that this institution has a character, a culture, and we intend to maintain and develop and foster it. This distinctive character of our organization is shown in the kind of integrity we apply as we go about our work. Much of the philosophy that caused our organization to come into being is worth preserving and maintaining, so we stress those principles. We are capturing this in an orientation program that every employee will have to go through. This is so everyone will know the absolute standards of performance and what our expectations are, and why these are so important to our success.

Samuel Armacost is the son of a onetime president of Redlands University. He earned an MBA at Stanford and has been a part of BankAmerica for over 20 years. He consciously puts himself out among his employees and seeks their opinions and ideas and then offers his in return. He is said to be nurturing open communication and mutual respect.

He calls it "creating an atmosphere where you don't shoot the messengers—you don't shout and scream when someone brings you bad news. You say, 'Thanks,' and ask what you should do about it."

In thinking about what business schools teach in the way of communication, he feels the stress in learning has been limited to skill aspects. He feels the art of sound communication needs to be approached from a broader perspective.

I'm not sure that the communication equation is being approached enough as a totality. We need to teach students of business to think through the impact of a decision, or what to recommend, say, in terms of the impact a change in advertising strategy could have on the marketplace.

I think we have to get outside into the big circle and look backwards, rather than focus on the small end of the tube always. The tendency has been to concentrate harder on skill enhancement aspects of communication rather than trying to start with the bigger issue of what it is we are trying to convey and accomplish. And then, you can more easily back into *how* you are going to say it.

Agreeing that business schools need to stress more the importance of the process of communication in successful management, he felt some real-life laboratory cases would help. His suggestion:

Why not give students a plant closing case and let them work on the communications that are needed? Have them write a memo on company policy for the closing. Then, put them in a room with six or eight hard-boiled union reps and let them see what it takes to convey their message. Or, find some real life examples where management is trying to deliver some messages to a group, and then take them out and let them stand in a crowd and see how it feels to be part of the audience. That's the essence of what I see needed to address communication education and training in a more straightforward way.

As for decision making at the top, Armacost emphasizes that the only way a CEO can solve problems and meet challenges is to have good information that presents a means of identifying what the actions are that need to be taken. Describing his personal technique in getting access to such insightful information, he says, "I try to cultivate various levels of the organization so I can cross-check attitudes and find out how different layers are perceiving different kinds of messages."

That's often a shattering experience. You find out that the message is not getting down to certain levels or is getting changed or revised. Unless you constantly check the process, you can think you are doing a great job when actually, little may be getting down past the first level of management.

I think you have to work very hard as a CEO not to be isolated, if only because people like to carry good news and they shy away from delivering the bad news. You must work hard at getting underneath the messages and finding out why and what people are saying. I try and learn why do they think what they think. Unless you do this digging, there's no way to draft a positive communication statement. I think those behavioral messages and colorations are important. We also have to be marketing-oriented in our communication.

That means getting out and transmitting the message that I've been giving internally and demonstrating that you have to listen to your customers. They ought to be the best source of feedback in terms of product enhancement and product needs. You have to talk to your customers and interface with them. It's fine to say that but I think you have to *do* it.

I spend really a vast portion of my time—both domestic and abroad—dealing with customers, meeting customers, accompanying account officers to meetings or contacts at levels that they presumed they did not have access to. I ask for business and I volunteer to be a spear carrier on closing deals. I respond to miscues on our part by asking that I see more than a carefully selected sample of complaints. Then I address those instances specifically and follow it up by making sure that various levels in our organization know that I watch and am interested in the problems we have rather than in just hearing about the successes. It takes a lot of time. But unless you're willing to invest that time, you can't expect others to do it for you.[3]

Armacost estimates that he spends over half of his executive time on communications. He says he has found the demand for information in BankAmerica is greater than he can possibly supply. "We're really a team-oriented organization and we're going to try a little more concentrated activity and focus on capturing a singular image and see if that will help get the message through."

Listening to Armocast talk, it is evident that the role of the CEO as communicator involves hard work and a certain amount of frustration as the leader sees his messages bent out of shape or misunderstood as they work their way down through a large organization. There are no easy answers. But the sincerity of the CEO's conviction that communication is critical to the future of the enterprise is a powerful instrument to achieve the goals set for the corporation.

How To Start

One logical starting point is to begin to bridge the gap between what business schools try to teach and what we know our future corporate leaders need to know. When asked, the vast majority of CEOs and senior managers say that the most valuable and lasting components of their formal education were the nontechnical, nonprofessional subjects in the liberal arts and humanities. Of course, it was the technical subjects that probably got them into the system in the first place. That important first job was usually gained because of the practical skills acquired from coursework in business, engineering, or science. Now many CEOs enjoy the fashionable luxury of looking back on their formal education and considering the value of college instruction in great books, works of art, music, and drama. This point seems clear: a good business education must represent a balance between study of professional subjects and study in the liberal arts and humanities. At present, many business schools have lost sight of that balance by allowing too large a proportion of the curriculum to fall to the technical side. Most important, study of the communication process and the acquisition of communication skills is either absent from the curriculum or not working at full potential.

The manager who takes the initiative to pick up the phone to talk with the business school dean at the local college or university will be guaranteed of getting some kind of positive response from that individual. It is time now, we are convinced, that a workable partnership be forthcoming.

One way to support unified thinking between education and the realistic needs of the business world is to set in motion an exchange program. Let six business school professors spend a few months as staff managers in the corporate suite. Let an equal number of corporate staff people enter the classroom and take over teaching functions for a semester. This kind of rich intermixing of ideas can develop mutuality of interest, improve communication, and, more important, strengthen the two-way intermesh of creative energies that lies at the heart of any cooperative effort.

This is no pipe dream. A colleague in London, Alan Eden-Green, former president, British Institute of Public Relations, was, with his CEO, Sir Leslie Smith, the change agent for a unique program in the United Kingdom to build closer understanding between Britain's lawmakers and the nation's industrialists.

Sir Leslie, as head of BOC International (formerly British Oxygen), was concerned about a gap of understanding between Parliamentarians and industrialists which was becoming increasingly apparent and dangerous. Analysis showed that only about 15 percent of MPs had any direct experience in industry. This visionary British business leader saw that what was needed was opportunity for individual MPs to get some practical experience in industry. Sir Leslie convened several meetings of senior officers of other companies, and from these discussions of the problem Eden-Green was able to put together an entirely new organization, the Industry and Parliament Trust Limited.

The Trust, which now has 28 companies in membership, has so far appointed 109 Parliamentarians as Fellows, each of whom undertakes a 25-day course spread over a year with one of the member companies studying industry first-hand. They learn how business decisions are made, what relationships are really like in industry, and how industry and Parliament interrelate. A reverse flow of information also takes place, with the Parliamentarians teaching industrialists about how Parliament functions and the various stages which a bill has to pass through before it becomes law.

Parallel organizations have now been formed in Holland, Norway, and Sweden. Eden-Green writes, "The point I would emphasize is that what was achieved was the direct result of the right kind of relationship and continuing dialogue between the CEO and his PR/public affairs adviser."[4]

Numerous efforts are already under way to bring academe and the authentic needs of the corporate world closer.[5] A number of U.S. corporations have established tuition assistance programs with educational institutions, such as Kimberly-Clark Corporation with the University of Wisconsin–Oshkosh and Polaroid Corporation with Rochester Institute of Technology. On a smaller scale, some corporations have participated actively in joint curriculum improvement efforts, through corporate-sponsored in-service activities such as General Electric's Educators-in-Industry program. A number of companies, such as RCA, Arthur D. Little, Control Data, Singer, and the Chrysler Learning Institute, provide instructional programs that compare very favorably with those offered traditionally by colleges and universities. In 1978, the American Council of Education launched the Business–Higher Education Forum, consisting of CEOs and college presidents who meet to consider mutually beneficial activities and explore avenues for joining forces.

But these are just a start. Despite considerable media coverage of such joint programs, too few are actually in operation providing substantial cooperative efforts. Many more are needed. This learning process is as vital for the educators of business as it is for the leaders of business. The street runs both ways—as does the communication.

In a quest for excellence in business and communication, there is much to be learned from the performance of William A. Hewitt, former chief executive of Deere & Company, who was the company's leader through 27 years of its biggest growth. In that time span from 1955 to 1982, Deere, with Hewitt's hand on the helm, grew from sales of $339 million to more than $5.4 billion and employment tripled.

Listen to some of William Hewitt's private thoughts on leadership, worker motivation, and teamwork. This is the stuff of which good communication is made.

> I believe that leadership and style are qualities that emerge like one's personality. Whatever their constituencies may be, leaders are persons who can move groups of people to action. Their real strength comes from their ability to foresee a need for change—not just change for change's sake, but change that is positive and innovative, the kind of change that will establish or maintain a position of leadership.

The job of a CEO is somewhat like that of a symphony orchestra conductor. There is absolutely no way and no reason why the conductor should try to be a better instrumentalist than each member of the orchestra. He must understand the music and know what the instruments are capable of doing. He must recognize when mistakes are being made. Then his job is to motivate people to play together and to play better. This should be done by example rather than by issuing edicts. And a good leader should give people the freedom to fail once in a while.

. . . the main point is that in this company we all need each other. Nobody accomplishes anything big by himself.[6]

In his communication of messages to Deere's employees, customers, stockholders, and all of its varied audiences, Hewitt's innate sense of beauty and the arts was used constantly. Here is how Ralph Reynolds, editor of *The Furrow,* Deere's remarkably successful external magazine for its dealers and farmer customers, has written of this renaissance leader-communicator:

You see, Hewitt admired and respected farmers, and in doing so he ascribed to them taste as cultivated and elevated as his own. He was never one to say, "I don't like that, but it's probably good enough for farmers." Instead his contention was, "I don't like that. Therefore it's not good enough for farmers." I view this as the ultimate compliment. I think many farmers and ex-farmers who know him will agree that Bill Hewitt's senses have always been attuned to the beauty of the countryside, and the deeply-held values of farm people. He expressed that over and over in what the company has designed, produced, and built.[7]

The renaissance in American corporate leadership can be a grassroots movement. It does not require a meeting between Charles L. Brown, chairman of AT&T, and Derek Bok, president of Harvard. It does require, however, that responsible and ambitious managers in small companies initiate contact with business teachers at local colleges and vice versa. The renaissance does not begin with giant multinational corporations, but with an individual: with you, the reader of this book. Whether one is the president of a small manufacturing company in California or the general manager of a grain mill in Nebraska, the superintendent of a saw mill in Oregon or a foreman on an assembly line in Michigan, the initiatives and opportunities are the same. All the principles presented here are ready to be applied and need not cost much in terms of money.

In many cases the budget is already being spent for communication but the results are not bankable. This waste of financial and human resources should no longer be tolerated.

The payoff will not be immediate. Once the process is begun, however, the benefits will be cumulative. And if the effort and resources committed are sufficient, the bountiful results will be measured well into the next century.

Notes

CHAPTER 1: The Present Crisis in American Corporate Leadership (pp. 3–12)

1. Details abound in numerous business periodicals. For a representative sample, see *Fortune,* March 9, 1981.
2. Reported in an interview with Deming, "U.S. Labor 'Has Surrendered to Japan,' " in the *Chicago Tribune,* November 8, 1981.
3. The most quoted of these surveys is Robert Quinn and Graham Staines, *The 1977 Quality of Employment Survey.* Ann Arbor, MI: University of Michigan, Survey Research Center, Institute for Social Research, 1979.
4. "Business Failures Hit Post-Depression High; Tide Expected to Swell," *Wall Street Journal,* May 24, 1982.
5. Karen W. Anderson, "The Erosion of American Industry," *New York Times,* August 8, 1982.
6. Kim Clark, "The Impact of Unionization on Productivity: A Case Study," *Industrial and Labor Relations Review,* Vol. 33, No. 4, 1980, pp. 451–469.
7. Alma Baron and Robert Witte, "The New Work Dynamic: Men and Women in the Work Force," *Business Horizons,* Vol. 23, August 1980, pp. 56–60. See also Lou Stanek, "Women in Management: Can It Be a Renaissance for Everybody?" *Management Review,* Vol. 69, November 1980, pp. 44–48.
8. Interview by Ronald Goodman with Malcolm C. Myers, December 28, 1982.
9. Interview by Ronald Goodman with George Holm, December 29, 1982.
10. Miyamoto Musashi, *A Book of Five Rings.* New York: Overlook Press, 1982.
11. "UAW Leaders Urge Early Contract Talks with GM, Ford in Bid to Halt Job Erosion," *Wall Street Journal,* December 14, 1981.

CHAPTER 2:   Image at the Top—Critical Role of the CEO (pp. 13–20)

1. *A Final Report on the Results from the GM Employee Survey,* General Motors Corporation, March 1974, p. 1.
2. *Ibid.,* p. 17.
3. Richard S. Ruch, "Job Satisfaction for Nonskilled Assembly Plant Employees: A Theoretical Paradigm and Secondary Analysis of Survey Data," Ph.D. dissertation, Rensselaer Polytechnic Institute, 1976. See also Richard S. Ruch, "A Path Analytic Study of the Structure of Employee Job Satisfaction: The Critical Role of Top Management," *Journal of Vocational Behavior,* Vol. 15, 1979, pp. 277–293.
4. "Special Report: Managing Human Resources/1982—a Strategy Briefing for Executives by the Opinion Research Corporation, New York City, December 7, 1982," *Behavioral Sciences Newsletter,* January 10, 1983, p. 1.
5. *Ibid.,* p. 3.
6. *Ibid.*
7. "Levity Helps Finance Chief for Chrysler," *Wall Street Journal,* May 14, 1981.

CHAPTER 3:   The Renaissance in Corporate Leadership (pp. 21–47)

1. Louis B. Lundborg, "Management Looks at Public Relations," Annual Conference, Public Relations Society of America, Denver, August 9, 1965.
2. Thomas J. Watson, Jr., speech delivered before the Annual Conference, Public Relations Society of America, New York, November 6, 1958.
3. "GM's Bonus Flap: 'The Timing Was Wrong,' " *Wall Street Journal,* April 3, 1982, editorial page.
4. Letter to Ronald Goodman from Ronald O. Woods, Manager, Internal Communications—North America, Public Relations Staff, General Motors Corporation, December 8, 1982.
5. "The Sloan Touch," *Saturday Review,* April 9, 1966.
6. "Firestone Tests Showed Tire Danger, Paper Says," *New York Times,* July 25, 1978.
7. "Firestone Signs '500 Recall'; Faces Fine," *Washington Post,* November 30, 1978.
8. Letter to Ronald Goodman from Bernard W. Frazier, Director of Government Relations, The Firestone Tire & Rubber Company, January 20, 1983.
9. Letter to Ronald Goodman from Jerry L. Sloan, Director, Corporate Information Office, Ford Motor Company, January 19, 1983.

10. "Killing a Product—Taking Rely Off Market Cost Procter & Gamble a Week of Agonizing," *Wall Street Journal,* November 3, 1980.

11. *Ibid.*

12. *Report of the Annual Meeting of Shareholders,* Procter & Gamble Company, October 14, 1980, p. 12.

13. Remarks of James E. Burke, Chairman, Johnson & Johnson, to the Associated Press Managing Editors Conference, San Diego, CA, November 12, 1982.

14. "Tylenol's Maker Shows How to Respond to Crisis," *Washington Post,* October 11, 1982.

15. "Rivals Go After Tylenol's Market, But Gains May Be Only Temporary," *Wall Street Journal,* December 2, 1982.

16. "The Tylenol Nightmare: How a Corporate Giant Fought Back," by Rick Atkinson, *Kansas City Times,* November 12, 1982.

17. "The Fight to Save Tylenol: The Inside Story of Johnson & Johnson's Struggle to Revive Its Most Important Product," by Thomas Moore, *Fortune,* November 29, 1982.

18. "The Tylenol Comeback," a special report from the editors of *Worldwide,* a publication of Johnson & Johnson Corporate Public Relations, December 1982.

19. Personal interview with Ronald Goodman, January 13, 1983.

20. Remarks by General Robert E. Wood at the "On to Chicago Banquet," of Sears, Roebuck and Co. Chicago, May 4, 1950, p. 3.

21. *Ibid.*

22. T. V. Houser, "Big Business and Its Publics," Section 2 in *Big Business and Human Values,* McKinsey Foundation Lecture Series, New York, 1957, p. 41.

23. James C. Worthy, "Code for Corporate Citizens," Sears Northern Ohio Personnel & Executive Conference, Cleveland, January 30, 1958.

24. Personal interview with Ronald Goodman, January 14, 1983.

25. Erwin D. Canham, "New Frontiers of Communication," Annual Conference, Public Relations Society of America, Miami, FL, November 4, 1959.

CHAPTER 4: Alienation and Love on the Job (pp. 51–64)

1. Melvin Seeman is regarded as the classic guru on the subject of alienation, at least by academicians. His landmark article, "On the Meaning of Work Alienation," was published in 1959 in the *American Sociological Review* (Vol. 24, pp. 783–791). Almost everything written on the subject since has been a rehash of Seeman's original thoughts. We depart from

Seeman's typology and approach this important topic from a different perspective.

2. Data to support Figures 4.1, 4.2 and 4.3 are widely available in the job satisfaction literature. Citations are available from a number of sources and we have taken the liberty of generalizing without listing them here. For some of our own citations, see Richard S. Ruch, "A Path Analytic Study of the Structure of Employee Job Satisfaction: The Critical Role of Top Management," *Journal of Vocational Behavior,* Vol. 15, 1979, pp 277–293.

3. Erich Fromm, *The Art of Loving.* New York: Harper & Row, 1956.

4. The KCRR model was first presented by Richard Ruch at the Second Japan–United States Business Conference, Tokyo, Japan, April 5, 1983. Richard first learned about KCRR from William E. Lynch, a philosopher and writer in Miami, Florida, who has used the model successfully for more than a decade in his family counseling practice. Copies of Dr. Lynch's pamphlet, *How to Love* (Miami, FL: By the author, 1974), may be obtained by writing to him at 4699 Ponce de Leon Blvd., Miami, FL 33146.

5. Ronald Goodman and Richard S. Ruch, "In the Image of the CEO," *Public Relations Journal,* February 1981, pp. 14–19. A similar finding has been common in recent years in corporate employee attitude surveys.

6. William Ouchi, *Theory Z.* Reading, MA: Addison-Wesley, 1981.

7. Joseph Zima and Ronald Smith, "Communication: Intermediary Agent for Meeting Personal and Organization Expectations," Annual Conference, International Communication Association, Phoenix, AZ, 1971.

CHAPTER 5:   Management Education and the MBA Myth (pp. 65–74)

1. This view, widely shared among CEOs and personnel executives across the country, was expressed in Richard Ruch's essay, "Humanizing the MBA," *Chronicle of Higher Education,* Vol. 20, No. 13, May 27, 1980.

2. Excerpts of address by Lewis H. Young to the graduating class of Fordham University Graduate School of Business Administration, "Notable and Quotable," *Wall Street Journal,* August 11, 1980.

3. John Slaughter made these remarks at a convocation presentation at Kansas State University, Manhattan, KS, February 26, 1981, as reported in "Education Crisis Stifles Development," *Kansas State Collegian,* February 27, 1981, p. 1.

4. Bong-Gon P. Shin and Larry C. Wall, "A Pilot Study of the Social Responsibility Concept: A Manager's Viewpoint." Center for Business

and Economic Research, Western Illinois University, Macomb, IL, Working Paper No. 1982–2, p. 1.

5. H. Gordon Fitch, "Business and the Humanities: Connections." University of Kansas, Lawrence, KS, School of Business Occasional Paper Series, Spring 1981, pp. 14–15.

6. Peter Drucker, "The Coming Changes in Our School Systems," *Wall Street Journal,* March 3, 1981, editorial page.

7. James L. Hayes, "The Ideal Business School Curriculum: An Executive's Viewpoint," speech delivered at Business and the Humanities: A National Conference, University of Kansas, Lawrence, KS, March 26, 1981.

8. Peter Cohen, *The Gospel According to the Harvard Business School.* New York: Penguin Books, 1974, p. 8.

9. S. I. Hayakawa, *Language and Thought in Action.* New York: Harcourt Brace Jovanovich, 1973, p. 109.

10. "The Money Chase," *Time,* May 4, 1981, p. 59.

11. James G. Gentry, "Feedback on the College of Business Administration," *Management Horizons,* Vol. 9, 1978, pp. 1–9. Also H. C. Edgeworth, "Business Communication and Colleges of Business," *ABCA Bulletin,* September 1978, pp. 34–37.

12. William V. Muse, "If All the Business Schools in the Country Were Eliminated, Would Anyone Notice?" *Collegiate News & Views,* Vol. 36, No. 3, Spring 1983, pp. 1–5.

13. For a detailed accounting, see F. E. Beckett, *College Composition: The Course Where a Student Doesn't Learn to Write.* New York: Calcon Press, 1974.

14. L. E. Pate and G. E. Merker, "Communication Apprehension: Implications for Management and Organizational Behavior," *Journal of Management,* Vol. 4, 1978, pp. 107–119.

15. Mary Munter, "Trends in Management Communication at Graduate Schools," *Journal of Business Communication,* Winter 1983, Vol. 20, No. 1, pp. 5–11.

16. Carl Sagan, *Dragons of Eden.* New York: Ballantine Books, 1977, p. 202.

17. Gerard G. Gold (ed.), *Business and Higher Education: Toward New Alliances.* San Francisco: Jossey-Bass, 1981.

CHAPTER 6:   The Classic Charade in Corporate Communication (pp. 75–88)

1. Chester Barnard, *The Functions of the Executive.* Cambridge, MA: Harvard University Press, 1938.

2. "The Corporate Image," *Business Week,* January 22, 1979.

3. "Ethics and the Corporation," *Wall Street Journal,* April 16, 1975, editorial page.

4. Ronald Goodman & Company, "Survey of Working Press in Iowa on Effectiveness of Hospital Communication," March 4, 1976. Also presented to the Iowa Society for Hospital Public Relations Directors, Des Moines, IA, March 17, 1976.

5. "People Are Key to 'Excellent' Companies," *Kansas City Star,* October 27, 1981. See also Thomas J. Peters and Robert A. Waterman, Jr., *In Search of Excellence: Lessons from America's Best-run Companies.* New York: Harper & Row, 1982.

6. " 'Big Jim' Is Watching at RMI Co., and Its Workers Like It Just Fine," *Wall Street Journal,* August 4, 1980.

7. "A Sad Saga Ends," *Tucson Citizen,* July 13, 1979.

8. *Jack O'Dwyer's Newsletter,* Vol. 12, No. 6, June 27, 1979. For a full review of Three Mile Island see Mike Gray and Ira Rosen, *The Warning.* New York: W. W. Norton & Co., 1982.

9. "Business Relations with the Press; Three Versions of the Way It Is," *Wall Street Journal,* July 6, 1981. See also pamphlet by David Finn, "The Business-Media Relationship: Countering Misconceptions and Distrust," Research & Forecast, Inc., New York, 1981.

10. Interview by Ronald Goodman with Dr. Dietrich L. Leonhard, Chicago, November 3, 1959.

11. Hyman G. Rickover, "Thoughts on the Presidency," *New York Times,* February 21, 1982.

12. "To the Class of '84—It's not as bad as it looks," *Des Moines Register,* October 19, 1980.

CHAPTER 7: The Myth of the New Communication Technology (pp. 89–96)

1. Personal interview with Ronald Goodman, January 11, 1983.

2. *Ibid.*

3. Ronald Goodman and Richard Ruch, "Research in Internal Communication," *Public Relations Journal,* Vol. 38, No. 7, July 1982, pp. 16–19.

4. Alfred McClung Lee, "The Long Struggle to Make Sociology Useful," *Public Relations Journal,* Vol. 38, No. 7, July 1982, pp. 8–11.

5. Abraham Lincoln, from the Lincoln-Douglas debate at Ottawa, IL, on August 21, 1858.

CHAPTER 8:   The Communication Audit—Company Communication on the Psychiatric Couch (pp. 99–113)

1. Based upon a similar model advanced by Rensis Likert in *The Human Organization: Its Management and Value.* New York: McGraw-Hill, 1967, p. 76.

2. See Charles Hampden-Turner, *Radical Man,* Cambridge, MA: Schenkman Publishing Co., 1970, pp. 184–192.

3. See Kurt Lewin, *Resolving Social Conflicts,* New York: Harper & Row, 1948. Also: Dorwin Cartwright and Alvin Zander, eds, *Group Dynamics.* New York: Harper & Row, 1968.

CHAPTER 9:   The Power of Leadership Through Human Communication (pp. 114–129)

1. Carl F. Frost, John H. Wakeley, and Robert A. Ruh, *The Scanlon Plan for Organization Development: Identity, Participation, and Equity.* Michigan State University Press, East Lansing, MI, 1974. See also Richard Ruch, *The Scanlon Plan at Herman Miller.* Zeeland, MI: Herman Miller, Inc., 1976.

2. Robert K. Greenleaf, *Servant Leadership: A Journey into Legitimate Power and Greatness.* New York: Paulist Press, 1977, p. 12.

3. Carmela C. Maresca and Leslie R. Wolfe, "Diet Center Gaining Market Weight," *Advertising Age,* May 3, 1982.

4. Personal conversation between Richard S. Ruch and Jim Liljenquist, January 3, 1983.

5. Gerald M. Goldhaber, Harry S. Dennis, Gary M. Richetto, and Osmo A. Wiio, *Information Strategies: New Pathways to Corporate Power.* Englewood Cliffs, NJ: Prentice-Hall, 1979, p. 21.

6. For further information see James Sloan Allen, *The Romance of Commerce and Culture: Capitalism, Modernism and the Chicago-Aspen Crusade for Cultural Reform* (Chicago: University of Chicago Press, 1983), and Sydney Hyman, *The Aspen Idea* (Norman, OK: University of Oklahoma Press, 1975).

7. Personal interview with the authors, May 11, 1982, in Manhattan, KS.

CHAPTER 10:   Making the Renaissance Happen (pp. 130–150)

1. David K. Easlick, "To See Ourselves As Others See Us," *Bell Telephone Magazine,* June 1981, pp. 20–21.

2. Personal interview with the authors, September 20, 1982, in Zeeland, MI.

3. Interview by the authors with Samuel H. Armacost, November 22, 1982.

4. Letter to Ronald Goodman from Alan Eden-Green, Director, Industry and Parliament Trust Limited, London, January 4, 1983.

5. For an informative discussion of collaborative research efforts between universities and industry, see Derek Bok, *Beyond the Ivory Tower.* Cambridge, MA: Harvard University Press, 1982, pp. 136–213.

6. "Interview: William A. Hewitt—The Quest for Excellence," *J. D. Journal,* Vol. 11, Winter 1982–83.

7. "He Looked Beyond the Bottom Line," *The Furrow,* November–December 1982.

Index